I0007866

SQL Programming

The Ultimate Guide with Exercises, Tips and Tricks to Learn SQL

by Damon Parker

Copyright 2019 by Damon Parker
All rights reserved

The content of this book may not be reproduce, duplicated or transmitted without direct written permission from the author or the publisher.

Under no circumstances will any blame or legal responsibility be held against the publisher or author, for any damages, reparation or monetary loss due the information contains within this book.

Legal Notice:
This book is copyright protected and is only for personal use. You cannot amend, distribute, sell, use or quote any part of this book without the consent of the author or the publisher.

Disclaimer Notice:
Please note the information contained within this document is for educational purpose only. All effort has been executed to present accurate, up to date and reliable, complete information. No warranties of any kind are declared or implied. Readers acknowledge that the author is not engaging in the rendering of legal, financial, medical or professional advice. The content within this book has been derived from various sources. Please consult a licensed professional before attempting any techniques outlined in this book. By reading this document, the reader agrees that under no circumstances is the author responsible for any losses, direct or indirect, which are incurred as a result of the use of information contained within this document, including, but not limited to, errors, omissions or inaccuracies.

Table of Contents

Introduction

Congratulations on downloading **SQL Programming:** *The Ultimate Guide with Exercises, Tips, and Tricks to Learn SQL,* and thank you for doing so.

The following chapters will discuss the foundational concepts of the Structured Query Language (SQL) to help you not only learn but master this data analysis language to extract information from the relational database management systems. This book is written to serve as your personal guide so you can efficiently and effectively use SQL to retrieve from and update information on SQL databases and servers, using the MySQL server for reference, which is one of the most widely used interface for relational database management.

The first chapter of this book titled *Introduction to SQL* will provide you an overview of the database management systems as well as different types of database management systems and their advantages. You will be introduced to the SQL language and the five fundamental types of SQL queries. In this chapter, you will learn the thumb rules for building SQL syntax or query. A variety of SQL data types that are a pre-requisite for learning SQL are provided in explicit detail.

In Chapter 2 titled, *Basic SQL Functions*, you will be introduced to the MySQL, which is a free and open-source relational database management system. A step by step walkthrough as well as installation of MySQL on your operating system(s) has been provided so you can easily download and install this free resource on your system. This will allow you to get hands-on practice utilizing all the practice exercises included in this book to master the SQL programming language. You will be learning how to generate a whole new database and subsequently create tables and insert data into those tables on the MySQL server. You will also learn the concept of temporary tables, derived tables and how you can generate a new table from a table already present in the database.

In Chapter 3 titled, *Advanced SQL Functions*, you will be learning about the SQL SELECT statements along with the various Data manipulation clauses such as ORDER BY and WHERE. The key concept of SQL Joins is provided in exquisite detail including different SQL JOIN functions such as INNER JOIN, LEFT JOIN and many more. The SQL Union function will also be explained along with the MySQL UNION and MySQL UNION ALL statements.

In Chapter 4 titled, *SQL Views and Transactions*, the concept of Database View in SQL has been explained, which is simply a virtual table defined using the SQL SELECT statements using the SQL JOIN clause(s). Some of the SQL view related statements explained in this chapter include CREATE VIEW, MERGE, TEMPTABLE, UNDEFINED, Updatable SQL Views, ALTER VIEW and CREATE OR REPLACE VIEW statements. The properties of SQL transactions as well as various SQL transaction statements with controlling clauses such as, START TRANSACTION, COMMIT, ROLLBACK among others are also explained in this chapter.

The last chapter titled, Database Security and Administration, mainly focuses on the user access privileges that are required to securely manage the data on a MySQL server. You will be walked through the entire process of creating new user accounts, updating the user password as well as granting and revoking access privileges to ensure that only permitted users have authorized and required access to the database.

There are plenty of books on this subject on the market, thanks again for choosing this one! Every effort was made to ensure it is full of as much useful information as possible; please enjoy!

Chapter 1:Introduction to SQL

A database could be defined as an organized collection of information or data, which can be stored electronically on a computer system and accessed as needed. A Database Management System (DBMS) can be defined as a program that allows end-user interactions with apps as well as the database for capturing and analyzing the data. It is an integrated computer software package enabling users to communicate with a number of databases and offering access to the information stored on the database. The DBMS offers multiple features that enable big volumes of data to be entered, stored and retrieved as well as offers methods for managing how the data can be organized. Considering this close association, the term database frequently refers to both databases as well as DBMS.

Existing DBMSs provide multiple features to manage and classify a database and its information into four primary functional groups as follows:

- **Data definition**–Definitions that represent the organization of data are created, modified and eliminated.
- **Update**–Inserting, modifying and deleting the actual data.

- **Retrieval**-Provision of data in a form that can be used directly or processed further by other applications. Data collected may be accessed in the same format as existing in the database or in a different format that can be acquired through alteration or combination of data sets from various databases.

- **Management**–User registration and tracking, data security enforcement, performance tracking, data integrity, competence control, and the recovery of data damaged by a certain event, for example, an accidental glitch in the system.

A database and its DBMS are in accordance with a given model database. The database system can be defined as a collection of the database, DBMS, and database model.

Database servers are physically connected computers that only run DBMS and associated software, holding real databases. Multiprocessor machines with extensive memory and RAID disk arrays utilized for long term storage of the data are called as database servers. If one of the disks fails, RAID can be used to recover the data. In a heavy volume transaction processing setting, hardware DB accelerator linked with single or multiple databases using the high-speed channels are being utilized. Most database applications have DBMS at their core. DBMS may be created with built-in network assistance around a custom multitasking kernel, but contemporary DBMSs typically use a normal operating system to offer the same functionalities.

As DBMS represents an important market, DBMS requirements are often taken into consideration by computers and storage providers for their production plans.

Databases and DBMSs may be grouped by on the basis of following parameters:

- The supported database models, for example, relational or XML databases.
- The variety of computers on they can operate on, for example, a cluster of servers linked to a wireless device.
- The programming language used to query the database, for example, SQL or XQuery.
- The internal engineering drives the efficiency, scalability, resiliency as well as safety of the system.

We will be primarily focusing on relational databases in this book, which pertains to the SQL language. In the beginning of the 1970s, IBM began to work on a prototype model based on the ideas of the computer scientist named Edgar Codd as System R. The first version was introduced in 1974 and 1975 and followed by work on multi-table systems that allowed splitting of the data so as to avoid storage of all the data as a single big slice for individual record. Customers tested subsequent multi-user versions in the late 1970s, after a standardized query language called SQL, was added to the database. Codd's concepts forced IBM to create a real version of "System R", called as "SQL / DS" and subsequently "Database 2 (DB2)."

The "Oracle database" developed by Larry Ellison, began from a distinct chain on the basis of the work published by IBM on System R. Whilst the implementation of Oracle V1 was finished in 1978, but it was with the release of Oracle Version 2 in 1979 that Ellison succeeded over IBM in entering the market.

For the further development of a new database, Postgres, now referred to as PostgreSQL, Stonebraker had used the INGRES classes. PostgreSQL is widely utilized for worldwide critical apps. The registrations of '.org' and '.info' domain names are primarily using PostgreSQL for data storage and similarly done by various big businesses and financial institutions. The computer programmers at the Uppsala University in Sweden, were also inspired by Codd's work and developed Mimer SQL in the mid-1970s. In 1984, this project was transitioned into an independent company.

In 1976, the entity relationship model was developed and became highly popular for designing databases as it produced a relatively better-known description compared to the preceding relational model. Subsequently, the structure of the entity-relationship was rebuilt into a data modeling construct, and their distinctions became insignificant.

Relational databases consist of a collection of tables that can be matched to one of the predetermined categories. Every table will have a minimum of one data category in a column and every row will contain some data instances for those categories that have been specified in the column. Relational databases have multiple names, such as Relational Database Management Systems (RDBMS) or SQL database. The Relational databases are mainly used in big corporate settings, with the exception of MySQL, which can also be used in web-based data storage.

All relation databases can be utilized for the management of transaction-oriented applications (OLTP). On the other hand, most non-relational databases in the classifications of Document Stores and Column Store, may also be used for OLTP, thus causing confusion between the two. OLTP databases can be considered operational databases, distinguished by regular quick transactions, including data updates, small volumes of data, and simultaneously processing hundreds and thousands of transactions, such as online reservations and banking apps.

Advantages of Database Management System

The DBMS can be described as a software system that is enabling its users in identification, development, maintenance, and regulated access to the data. It allows end customers to generate information in the database as well as to read, edit and delete desired data. It can be viewed as a layer between the information and the programs utilizing that data.

DBMS offers several benefits in comparison to the file-based data management system. Some of these advantages are listed below:

- **Reduction in the redundancy of data** - The file-based DBMS contains a number of files stored in a variety of location on a system and even across multiple systems. Due to this, several copies of the same file can often result in data redundancy. This can be easily avoided in a database since there is only a single database holding all the data and any modifications made to the database are immediately reflected across the entire system. Hence, there is no possibility that duplicate information will be found in the database.
- **Seamless data sharing** - Users can share all existing data with each other found within a database. Different levels of authorizations exist within the

database for selective access to the information. Therefore, it is not possible to share the information without following the proper authorization protocols. Multiple remote users can concurrently access the database and share any desired information as needed.

- **Data integrity** - The integrity of data implies that the information in the database is reliable and accurate. The integrity of data is very crucial as a DBMS contains a variety of databases. The information contained in all of these databases is available to all the users across the board. It is therefore essential to make sure that all the databases and customers have correct and coherent data available to them at all times.

- **Data security** - Data security is vital in the creation and maintenance of a database. Only authorized users are allowed to access the database by authenticating their identity using a valid username and password. Unauthorized users cannot, under any conditions, be permitted to access the database, as it infringes upon the data integrity rules.

- **Privacy** - The privacy rule in a database dictates that only authorized users are allowed to access the database on the basis of the predefined privacy constraints of the database. There are multiple database access levels and only permitted data can be viewed by the user. For example, various access limitations on the social networking sites for accounts that a user may want to access.

- **Backup and Recovery** -DBMS is capable of generating automated backup and recovery of the database. As a result, the users are not required to backup data regularly since the DBMS can efficiently handle this. In addition, it restores the database to its preceding state in case of any technical errors or system failure.

- **Data Consistency** - In a database, the consistency of data is guaranteed due to the lack of any redundant data. The entire database contains all data consistently, and all the users accessing the database receive the same data. In addition, modifications to the database are instantly reported to all the users to avoid any inconsistency of the existing data.

Structured Query Language

In the context of relational databases, it is considered a standard user and application program interface. In 1986, SQL was incorporated into the "American National Standards Institute (ANSI)," and in 1987, it was added to the "International Organization for Standardization (ISO)." Since then, the standards are constantly being improved and are endorsed by all mainstream commercial relational DBMSs (with different extents of compliance).

For the relational model, SQL was one of the initial commercial languages, even though it is distinct from the relational structure in certain aspects, according to Codd. For instance, SQL allows an organization to create and update data rows and columns. The relational databases are highly extensible. After the initial database has been created, a new data category can be easily introduced without needing to alter any current apps.

Types of SQL Queries

Database languages are defined as special-purpose languages, that enable execution of one or more of the tasks listed below and often called as sublanguages:

Data definition language (DDL) – It is used to define the types of data including its creation, modification, or elimination as well as the relationships among them.

Data manipulation language (DML) –Only after the database is created and tables have been built using DDL commands, the DML commands can be used to manipulate the data within those tables and databases. The convenience of using DML commands is that they can readily be changed and rolled back if any incorrect modifications to the data or its values have been made. The DML commands used to perform specific tasks are:

- **Insert** – For insertion of new rows in the table.
- **Update**–For modification of the data values contained in the rows of the table.
- **Deletion** – For deletion of selected rows or complete table within the database.
- **Lock** – To define the user access to either read only or read and write privilege.
- **Merge** – To merge a couple of rows within a table.

Data control language (DCL) – As the name indicates, the DCL commands pertain to data control problems in a database. DCL commands provide users with unique database access permissions and are also used to define user roles as applicable. There are two DCL commands that are frequently used:

- **Grant** – To give access permissions to the users.
- **Revoke** – To remove the access permission given to the users.

Data query language (DQL) – DQL comprises of a single command that drives data selection in SQL. In conjunction with other SQL clauses, the SELECT command is used for the collection and retrieval of data from databases or tables based on select user-applied criteria. A**"SELECT"**

statement is used to search for data and computing derived information from the table and/or database.

Transaction control language (TCL) – As indicated by its name, TCL administers transaction-related issues and problems in a database. They are used to restore modifications made to the original database or confirm them.
Roll back implies the modifications Undo, and Commit means the modifications Apply. The 3 main TCL commands available are:

- **Rollback** – Used to cancel or undo any updates made in the table or database.
- **Commit** – Used to deploy or apply or save any updates made in the table or database.
- **Save point** – Used to temporarily save the data in the table or database.

Database languages are limited to a specific data model as reflected in the examples below:

- **SQL** – It offers functions that allow you to define the data, manipulate the data as well as query the data as a unified language.
- **OQL**–This modeling language standard for objects was developed by the "Object Data Management Group."This

language inspired the development of other modern query languages such as JDOQL and EJBQL.

- **XQuery** – This standard query language for XML was introduced by XML database technologies. The relational databases with these capabilities like Oracle and DB2, as well as XML processors.

SQL SYNATX

The picture below depicts the most common syntax (code structure that can be understood by the server) of a SQL query. Before we jump into the actual SQL commands that you can execute for a hands-on learning experience. Here are some thumb rules that you must memorize first:

1. A semicolon must be used at the end of each command.
2. A keyword must be used at the beginning of the command. You will learn all the keywords as you progress through this book.
3. The case structure of the alphabets is irrelevant to the commands.
4. You must remember the name or title of the tables and databases, used at the time of creation and make sure you always use those specific names for all your commands.

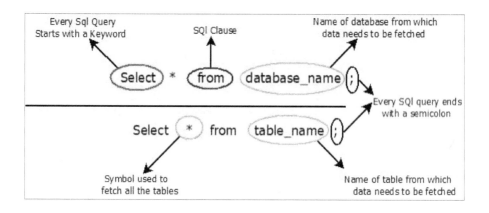

SQL Data Types

Another important concept in learning SQL, is the various data types that are required to define the types of data value to be inserted in specific columns. The commonly used data types are listed in the table below:

DATA TYPE	DESCRIPTION
char(size)	This is used to define a fixed length character string. The size of the data value can be specified using desired number in the parenthesis as shown. Maximum allowed size is 255 characters.
varchar(size)	This is used to define a variable length character string. The size of the data value

	can be specified using desired number in the parenthesis as shown. Maximum allowed size is 255 characters.
number(size)	This is used to define a numerical value with a specific number in parenthesis. The max number of digits in the column can be specified using desired number in the parenthesis as shown.
date	This is used to define a date value for pertinent column.
number(size,d)	This is used to define a numerical value with a specific number in parenthesis. The max number of digits in the column can be specified using desired number in the parenthesis, along with the no. of digits on the right of the decimal, as shown by the alphabet d.

Data Definition Language (DDL)

As the Codasyl database model was introduced, the term data definition language was coined. The concept of DDL required the database scheme to be developed in a syntax that described the record, field, and set of the user data models. Subsequently,

DDL was considered a subset of SQL used to declare tables, columns, data types, and constraints. The third major revision of SQL, called SQL – 92, laid the foundation for manipulation languages and info tables to execute queries on schema. In SQL – 2003, the data tables were described as SQL/Schemata.

DDL can be used to make or perform modifications to the physical structure of the desired table in a given database. All such commands can be inherently auto committed upon execution, and all modifications to the table are immediately reflected and stored across the database. Here are the most known and widely used DDL commands:

- **Create** – For creation of new table(s) or an entire database.
- **Alter** – To modify the data values of records that have been created for a table.
- **Rename** – To change the name of the table(s)or the database.
- **Drop** – To delete the table(s) from a database.
- **Truncate** – To delete an entire table from the database.

Now, we will explore various uses of these DDL commands to execute required operations. For ease of learning all the fixed codes or keywords will be written in CAPITAL LETTERS, so you can easily differentiate between the dummy data and command syntax.

SQL CREATECommand

Usage– As the name suggests, CREATE command is primarily used to build database(s) and table(s). This always tends to be the first step in learning SQL.

Syntax:

CREATE DATABASE db_name;

CREATE TABLE tab_name;

CREATE TABLE tab_name (col1 datatyp, col2 datatyp, col3 datatyp,....,);

Examples:

Let's assume you would like to create a database named as db_baseball, which contains one table that stores details of the teams called team_details and another table that stores details of the players called player_details.

The first step here would be to build the desired database, with the use of the command below:

CREATE DATABASE db_baseball;

Now, that you have your database in the system, use the command below to create desired tables:

CREATE TABLE team_details;

CREATE TABLE player_details;

If you wanted to create the table player_details with some columns like player_firstname with column size as 15, player_lastname with column size as 25 and player_age. You will use the command below:

*CREATE TABLE player_details (*player_firstname varchar (15), player_lastname varchar (25), player_age int*);*

Remember the size of the varchar data type can be mentioned in the statement with the maximum size as255 characters and in case the column size has not been specified, the system will default you to the maximum size

Hands-on Exercise

For exercise purposes, imagine that you are a brand-new business owner and looking to hire some employees. Now, you would first have to create a database for your company, let's name your company Health Plus and create a database named database_HealthPlus. You can then add a table titled New_Employees with columns to StoreEmployees' FirstName, LastName, JobTitle, Age and Salary.

Use your discretion and write your SQL statements first!

Now you can verify your statement against the right command as given below:

CREATE DATABASE db_HealthPlus;

CREATE TABLE New_Employees (employee_firstname varchar, employee_lastname varchar, employee_jobtitle varchar, employee_age int, employee_salary int);

SQL ALTER command

Usage– This command is primarily used to add a column, remove a column, add different data constraints and remove predefined data constraints.

Data Constraints – In terms of SQL, constraints are nothing, but specific rules applied to the data in the table. They can be applied at a column level, which is only applicable to the selected column or at a table level, which is applicable to all table columns. They limit the types of data values that are allowed to be entered in the table, to ensure the accuracy and reliability of the data. Violating these constraints will abort the command that you are trying to execute.

The data constraints can be added while creating the table (with the CREATE command) or once the table has been generated (utilizing the ALTER command).

The most widely used SQL constraints are:

- **NOT NULL** –It is utilized to make sure that the column always contains a value and does not hold a NULL value. Meaning, a new record cannot be added or a record that already exists cannot be modified if there are no values added to this column.

- **UNIQUE** - This constraint is used to make sure that every single data value in a column is distinct from one another.

- **PRIMARY KEY** - This constraint is essentially a merge of the UNIQUE and NOT NULL constraints. It serves as a unique identifier for each record in the table, which is required to contain a data value. Only one primary key can be indicated for individual tables.

- **FOREIGN KEY** - This constraint serves as a unique identifier for a record existing in a different table that has been linked to the table you are working on. This helps in aborting commands that will break the link between the two tables i.e., invalid data cannot be added to the foreign key column as it has to be a value as contained in the table that is holding that specific column.

- **CHECK** - This constraint is used to make sure that all the data values in a column meet a specific condition and are limited to the predefined value range. Applying Check constraint on a column will allow only select values to be added to that column. However, applying Check constraint on a table will put restrictions on the values that are added in the specified column, as dictated by the values specified in other columns of a row.

- **DEFAULT** –It is utilized to designate a default data value for a specific column in case no other value has been specified for that column.

- **INDEX** - This constraint is utilized to create and retrieve data values at a quick pace, using indexes that are not visible to the users. This should only be used for columns that will be searched more frequently than the others.

Syntax:

Addition ofColumns

ALTER TABLE tab_name
ADD col_namedtype;

DroppingColumn

ALTER TABLE tab_name
DROP col_name;

Addition of Not Null Constraint

ALTER TABLE tab_name
MODIFY col_namedtype NOT NULL;

Addition of Unique Constraint

ALTER TABLE tab_name
ADD UNIQUE col_name;

Addition of Primary Key Constraint

ALTER TABLE tab_name
ADD PRIMARY KEY col_name;

Addition of Foreign Key Constraint

ALTER TABLE tab_name
ADD FOREIGN KEY (col_name) REFERENCES tab_name
(col_name);

Addition of Check Constraint

ALTER TABLE tab_name
ADD CHECK(col_name<= 'numeric value');

Addition ofDefaultConstraint

ALTER TABLE tab_name
ADD CONSTRAINT (col_name) DEFAULT 'data_value' FOR
(col_name);

AddingIndexConstraint

CREATE INDEX index_name
ON tab_name (col1, col2, ...,);

DroppingNot NullConstraint

ALTER TABLE tab_name
DROP CONSTRAINT col_namedtype;

DroppingUniqueConstraint

ALTER TABLE tab_name
DROP CONSTRAINT col_namedtype;

DroppingPrimary KeyConstraint

ALTER TABLE tab_name
DROP PRIMARY KEY;

DroppingForeign KeyConstraint

ALTER TABLE tab_name
DROP FOREIGN KEY(col_name);

DroppingCheckConstraint

ALTER TABLE tab_name
DROP CHECK (col_name);

DroppingDefaultConstraint

ALTER TABLE tab_name
ALTER COLUMN (col_name)DROP DEFAULT;

DroppingIndexConstraint

DROP INDEX tab_name.indx_name;

Examples:

Now, assume that you would like to alter the player_details table, that was generated in the section above. To add a column titled player_ID and then drop the player_age column, you could execute the commands below:

ALTER TABLE player_details
ADD player_ID *number;*

ALTER TABLE player_details
DROP player_age;

Let's now look at how various constraints can be added with the player_details table!

You can specify that the column player_firstname has the Not Null constraint. The column player_lastname is unique. The primary key can be specified as column player_IDs, which will then become the foreign key in our other table titled team_details. We can define the check constraint on player_age to make sure all the values entered are above or equal to 20. We can also use the default value for player_age column as 20. Since, we will be frequently using the player_lastname column, let's add an index to it.

Step 1:
ALTER TABLE player_details
MODIFY player_firstname *varchar (15) NOT NULL;*

Step 2:
ALTER TABLE player_details
ADD UNIQUE player_lastname;

Step 3:

ALTER TABLE player_details

ADD PRIMARY KEY player_IDs;

Step 4:

ALTER TABLE team_details

*ADD FOREIGN KEY (*player_IDs*) REFERENCES* player_details

(player_IDs*);*

Step 5:

ALTER TABLE player_details

ADD CHECK (player_age<= 20);

Step 6:

ALTER TABLE player_details

ADD CONSTRAINT (player_age) DEFAULT '20' FOR

(player_age);

Step 7:

CREATE INDEX idx_name

ON player_details(player_lastname,player_firstname*);*

Now, let's drop all these constraints we just defined above, in the same order.

Step 1:

ALTER TABLE player_details
DROP CONSTRAINT player_firstname *varchar (15) NOT NULL;*

Step 2:

ALTER TABLE player_details
DROP CONSTRAINT player_lastname;

Step 3:

ALTER TABLE player_details
DROP PRIMARY KEY;

Step 4:

ALTER TABLE team_details
*DROP FOREIGN KEY (*player_IDs*);*

Step 5:

ALTER TABLE player_details
DROP CHECK (player_age);

Step 6:

ALTER TABLE player_details
ALTER COLUMN (player_age) DROP DEFAULT;

Step 7:

DROP INDEX player_details.*idx_name;*

Hands-on Exercise

For exercise purposes, we will continue to use the database_HealthPlus that we created in the previous section, which contains a table titled New_Employees with columns to store "Fst Name," "Lst Name," "Job Title," "Age" and "Salary" of the employee.

Now, let's add another table to this database titled Current_Employees. Then add a new column for employee ID which will be the primary key for table New_Employees and foreign key for Current_Employees. The salary column can be dropped for this exercise.

Make the column for the first name as Not Null and last name as Unique. Add a check constraint on the employee age column as equals or greater than 21. Then define its default value as 21. And lastly, indicate an index for the last name column to the New_Employees table.

****Use your discretion and prep your SQL statements first!****

Now you can verify your statement against the right command as given below:

Step 1:
CREATE TABLE Current_Employees (employee_fstname varchar, employee_lstname varchar, employee_jobtitl varchar, employee_age int, employee_salary int*);*

Step 2:
ALTER TABLE New_Employees
ADD employee_IDs *number;*

Step 3:
ALTER TABLE New_Employees
DROP employee_salary;

Step 4:
ALTER TABLE New_Employees
ADD PRIMARY KEY employee_IDs;

Step 5:
ALTER TABLE Current_Employees
ADD FOREIGN KEY (employee_ID*) REFERENCES*
New_Employees (employee_IDs*);*

Step 6:

ALTER TABLE New_Employees

MODIFY employee_fstname *varchar NOT NULL;*

Step 7:

ALTER TABLE New_Employees

ADD UNIQUE employee _lstname;

Step 8:

ALTER TABLE New_Employees

ADD CHECK (employee _age <= "21");

Step 9:

ALTER TABLE New_Employees

ADD CONSTRAINT (employee _age) DEFAULT '21' FOR

(employee_age);

Step 10:

CREATE INDEX idx_name

ON New_Employees(employee_lstname);

Viola!Now you are tasked to drop all these constraints and then add the salary column back to the New_Employees table.

Use your discretion and write your SQL statements first!

Now you can verify your statement against the right command as given below:

Step 1:
ALTER TABLE New_Employees
DROP PRIMARY KEY;

Step 2:
ALTER TABLE Current_Employees
*DROP FOREIGN KEY (*employee_IDs*);*

Step 3:
ALTER TABLE New_Employees
*DROP CONSTRAINT employee_*fstname *varchar NOT NULL;*

Step 4:
ALTER TABLE New_Employees
DROP CONSTRAINT employee_*lstname;*

Step 5:
ALTER TABLE New_Employees
DROP CHECK (employee _age);

Step 6:
ALTER TABLE New_Employees
ALTER COLUMN (employee_age) DROP DEFAULT;

Step 7:

DROP INDEX New_Employees.*idx_name;*

Step 8:

ALTER TABLE New_Employees
ADD employee_salary *number;*

SQL DROP DATABASECommand

Usage– This command is primarily used to delete an already existing SQL database.

Syntax:

DROP DATABASE db_name;

Examples:

Let's assume you would like to delete the database database_baseball for any business reason like irrelevant data in the database or duplicate databases etc.

You can simply use the command below and the entire database will be wiped out from the system.

DROP DATABASE db_baseball;

Hands-on Exercise

For exercise purposes, imagine that your company Health Plus has gone under or renamed, and you want to discard all the data you have available related to the company. What would you do?

Use your discretion and write your SQL statements first!

Now you can verify your statement against the right command as given below:

DROP DATABASE db_HealthPlus;

SQL CREATE VIEWCommand

Usage– This command is primarily used to generate a virtual view of the tables on the basis of the result-set of a SQL command. The view resembles an actual database table, in that it also has columns and rows, but the data values are called from an individual or multiple table(s) using "WHERE" and "JOIN."SQL Views are used to enhance the structure of the data making it more user-friendly.

In SQL, the WHERE function is used to selectively filter the data or records on the basis of specific conditions. It is a highly versatile function and can also be used with other SQL statements including UPDATE and DELETE.

Only the latest and greatest data will be used for the generation of a view!

Syntax:

CREATE VIEW vw_name AS
SELECT col1, col2, ...
FROM tab_name
WHERE condtn;

Examples:

Let's go back to the database database_baseball and assume you would like to view details of the players who are 25 years old.

You can simply use the command below and view desired information.

CREATE VIEW young_playersAS
SELECT player_fstname, player_lstname

FROM player_details
WHERE player_age = '25';

Hands-on Exercise

For exercise purposes, imagine that your company Health Plus is undergoing an organizational change and you would like to view a list of all the employees with the job title as managers.

Use your discretion and write your SQL statements first!

Now you can verify your statement against the right command as given below:

CREATE VIEW employee_mgrsAS
SELECT employee_fstname, employee_lstname
FROM Current_Employees
WIIERE employee_jobtitle= 'manager';

Chapter 2: Basic SQL Functions

MySQL has always been a popular open source SQL based RDMS, which is available for free. In 1995, a Swedish company called MySQL AB originally developed, marketed and licensed the MySQL data management system, that was eventually acquired by Sun Microsystems (now called Oracle Co.). MySQL is a LAMP software stack web application component, an acronym for "Linux, Apache, MySQL, Perl / PHP / Python." Several database-controlled web apps, like "Drupal", "Joomla", "PhpBB", and "WordPress" are using "MySQL."It is one of the best applications for RDBMS to create various online software applications and has been used in development of multiple renowned websites including Facebook, YouTube, Twitter and Flickr.

MySQL has been used with both C and C++. MySQL can be operated on several systems, including "AIX, BSDi, FreeBSD, HP-Ux, eComStation, i5/OS, IRIX, Linux, macOS, Microsoft Windows, NetBSD, Novell NetWare, OpenSolaris, OS/2 Warp, QNX, Oracle Solaris, Symbian, SunOS, SCO OpenServer, SCO UnixWare, Sanos and Tru64." Its SQL parser is developed in "yacc" and it utilizes an in house developed lexical analyzer. A MySQL port for OpenVMS has also been developed. Dual-license distribution is utilized for the MySQL server and its client libraries, which are available under version 2 of the GPL or a proprietary license. Additional free assistance is accessible on various IRC blogs and channels. With its MySQL Enterprise goods, Oracle is also providing paid support for their software. The range of services and prices vary. A number of third-party service providers, including MariaDB and Percona, offer assistance and facilities as well.

MySQL has been given highly favorable feedback from the developer community and reviewers have noticed that it does work exceptionally well in most cases. The developer interfaces exist and there's a plethora of excellent supporting documentation, as well as feedback from web locations in the real world. MySQL has also been successfully passed the test of a stable and fast SQL database server using multiple users and threads.

MySQL can be found in two editions: the "MySQL Community Server" (open source) and the "Enterprise Server," which is proprietary. "MySQL Enterprise Server" differentiates itself on the basis of a series of proprietary extensions that can be installed as server plug-ins, but nonetheless share the numbering scheme of versions and are developed using the same basic code.

Here are some of the key characteristics provided by MySQL v5.6:

- A largest subset of extensions and ANSI SQL-99 are supported by this version along with cross platforms.
- Stored procedures use procedural languages that are completely aligned with SQL/PSM.
- Cursors and triggers, views that can be updated, support for SSL; caching of queries; nested SELECT statements, integrated support for replication and info schema.
- Online Data Definition Language with the use of the InnoDB Storage Engine.
- Performance Schema that is capable of collecting and aggregating stats pertaining to monitor server executions and query performances.
- A set of options pertaining to SQL Mode for controlling runtime behavior, includes restrictive mode for improved adherence to SQL standards.
- "X/Open XA distributed transaction processing (DTP)" supports 2 phases committed with the use of the default InnoDB engine.
- Any transaction with save points while using the default engine can be supported by the "NDB Cluster Storage Engine."

- The replication may not be synchronous: owner employee from an owner to multiple employees or multiple owners to one employee.
- The replication may be partially synchronous: owner to employee replication where the owner awaits replication.
- The replication may be completely synchronous: Multi-owner replication can be supplied in MySQL Cluster.
- The replication may be virtually synchronous: groups of MySQL servers that are managed on their own with multi owner support that could be done with the use of the "Galera Cluster" or the integrated plug-in for group replication.
- The index of the full text and search capability, integrated database library, support for Unicode.
- The tables can be sectioned with the pruning of sections in the optimizer.
- MySQL Cluster allows for clustering of data that has not been shared.
- A number of storage engines that allow selection of the most effective engine for every table.
- The groups can be committed, and various transactions can be gathered from a number of connections together to raise the number of commitments made every second.

User Interfaces for MySQL

A graphical user interface (GUI) is a kind of interface that enables user interactions with software programs and electronics utilizing graphics, icons, buttons, and other indicators including but not limited to features supporting notations in lieu of navigation driven by text and text-based interfaces. GUIs are considered very easy to learn in comparison to the "command-line interfaces (CLIs)," where command must be entered on your keypad. MySQL offers a variety of interfaces that you can leverage to best meet your need. Some of the widely popular MySQL interfaces are:

MySQL Workbench

It is considered as the built-in environment for MySQL database, created by "MySQL AB," and allows the user supervision of MySQL graphically as well as the designing of the databases visually. It has substituted MySQL GUI Tools, which was the preceding software suite. MySQL Workbench enables users to perform database designing& model creation, SQL implementation, which was replaced by the Query Browser and Database admin, which was replaced by the MySQL Admin. These functionalities are also available from other third-party applications, but MySQL Workbench is still regarded as the official MySQL front end. MySQL Workbench can be downloaded from the official MySQL website, in two separate versions: a regular free and open source community version, and a proprietary standard version, which continues to expand and enhance the community version feature set.

phpMyAdmin

It is another open source application which is available for free and developed in PHP programming language, that allows use of a web browser to manage MySQL administration. It allows undertaking of multiple functions such as generation, modification, or deletion of database, table, field, or row by running SQL queries as well as management of users and permissions. phpMyAdmin is easily accessible in whopping 78 different languages and managed by The phpMyAdmin Project. The data can be imported as CSV or SQL and used with a set of predefined features to convert stored data into a desirable format, such as representing BLOB data as pictures or download links.

Adminer

Adminer (previously referred to as phpMinAdmin) is another open and free source MySQL front end for maintaining information in the MySQL databases. The release of version 2, the Adminer can also be used on PostgreSQL, SQLite and Oracle databases. The Adminer can be used to manage several databases with multiple CSS skins that are easily accessible. It is supplied under the Apache License or GPL v2 as a single PHP file. Jakub Vrána, began developing Adminer, in July 2007, as a lightweight option to the original phpMyAdmin application.

ClusterControl

It is defined as a holistic MySQL management system or GUI for managing, monitoring, scaling and deploying versions of MySQL from an individual interface. It has been engineered by "Severalnines." Its community version can be accessed for free and allow deployment and tracking of the MySQL instances, directly by the user. Advanced characteristics such as load balance, backup and restoration, among other are additional features that can be paid for.

Database Workbench

Database Workbench application was created by UpScene Productions, for the creation and management of various relational databases that are interoperable within separate database systems, using SQL. Databases Workbench can support several database systems and offers a cross-database tool for computer programmers with a similar interface and production environment, for a variety of databases. The relational databases that can be supported by Database Workbench are: Oracle, SQL Anywhere, Firebird, Microsoft SQL Server, NexusDB and many more. The version 5 of Database Workbench can be operated on Windows systems that are either 32-bit or 64-bit as well as on Linux, FreeBSD, or MacOS operating systems by leveraging the Wine application.

DBeaver

DBeaver is an open source and free software application marketed under Apache License 2.0, used as a database administration tool and a SQL client with the source code hosted on GitHub. DBeaver incorporates extensive assistance for the following databases: "MySQL and MariaDB, PostgreSQL, Oracle, DB2 (LUW), Exasol, SQL Server, Sybase, Firebird, Teradata, Vertica, Apache Phoenix, Netezza, Informix, H2, SQLite and any other JDBC or ODBC driver database."

DBEdit

It is a database editor capable of connecting to MySQL, Oracle and other databases that supports a JDBC driver. It is importance that SourceForge hosts the source code of this software. It is also defined as open source software, which is available for free under the GNU license. It is available on Windows, Linux and Solaris.

HeidiSQL

HeidiSQL, used to be known as "MySQL Front," is another open source application which is available for free and serves as a front end for MySQL, operable with MariaDB, Percona Server, Microsoft SQL Server and PostgreSQL. German computer scientist Ansgar Becker and several other contributors at Delphi, developed the HeidiSQL interface. To operate HeidiSQL databases, customers need to log in and create a session to a MySQL server locally or remotely with acceptable credentials. This session enables the users to develop a connection, in management of the database on the MySQL server and to disconnect from the server once they have completed their task. HeidiSQL function set is suitable for most popular and sophisticated activities pertaining to the database, table and data records, but it continues to actively grow towards the complete feature desired in a MySQL user interface.

LibreOffice Base

LibreOffice Base enables databases to be created and managed, forms to be prepared and reports providing simple access to information for the end-users. It also serves as an interface for different database systems like Microsoft Access, MySQL, OBDC info source, Access databases like JET and many more.

Navicat

It is a software that enables management of databases using graphics and coding programs for Oracle, MySQL, MariaDB, and other databases that have been manufactured by PremiumSoftCyberTech Ltd. It has a graphical user interface similar to the Microsoft Internet Explorer and supports various local and remote database connections. It has been designed to satisfy the demands of a range of customers, from database admins and developers to various corporations that are serving the public and share data with their partner companies. Navicat is a cross-platform software that can be operated on systems such as Microsoft Windows, OS X, and Linux. Once the software has been purchased, the user can select one of the available eight languages to work with their software, which are: Mandarin, Japanese, French, German, and many more.

Sequel Pro

It is another free and open source Macintosh operating system software that can be operated locally or remotely with MySQL databases and hosted on SourceForge. It utilizes the freemium model, which effectively provides Gratis users with most of the fundamental features. These applications need to be managed by a SQL Table itself. For newer unicode, it can manage the latest fun UTF-8 functions as well as having various GB tables with little to no difficulty.

SQLBuddy

SQLBuddy is a web-based open-source software published in PHP that manages MySQL and SQLite administration using a web browser. The objective of this design is easy software set-up and an enhanced and convenient interface for the users.

SQLyog

SQLyog is another MySQL GUI application which is available for free but also offers paid software versions of their platform. There is a spreadsheet resembling interface that allows data manipulation (e.g. insert, update and delete) to be accomplished easily.

Its editor offers multiple choices for automatic formatting such as syntax highlighting. A query can be used to manipulate both raw table data and outcome set. Its search function utilizes Google-like search syntax, which can be translated into SQL for users transparently. It is provided with a backup utility to execute unmonitored backups.

Toad

It was developed by Dell Software, as a computer application utilized by database programmers, database admins as well as data analysts, using SQL to operate on both relational and non-relational databases. Toad can be used with numerous databases and environments. It can be easily installed on all Windows operating systems such as Windows 7,Windows Vista, Server, XP and many more. A Toad Mac Edition has also been recently published by the Dell Software and is offered as a business version and trial / freeware version. The freeware version of Toad can be accessed from the ToadWorld.com community.

Webmin

Webmin was originally developed as an online system configuration software for Unix based systems, but the newer versions are available for installation and can be operated on Windows operating system as well. It allows customization of internal OS configurations such as disk quotas, utilities, users and open sourced applications such as MySQL, Apache HTTP Server among others that can be modified and controlled.

Webmin is primarily built on Perl, and one that runs as its own internet server and process. For communication, it would default to the TCP port 10000 and configured to utilize SSL (when OpenSSL has already been installed on the system with all Perl modules that are needed for execution). It is developed around modules that have an interface with the Webmin server and the configuration files. This makes adding latest features much more convenient. Because of the modular design of Webmin, custom plug-ins can be created for desktop setup for those who are keen. Webmin also enables control on many devices on the same subnet or LAN via one comprehensive user interface, or seamless connection to other Webmin hosts.

Installing MySQL on Linux/UNIX

MySQL should be installed using RPM on the Linux system. The following RPMs are accessible on the MySQL AB official site for download:

- **MySQL**–Its database server is used for management of the tables within a database, controlling the user access and processing the SQL statement.
- **MySQL bench** – These are the programs used to test and create a benchmark for the database servers.
- **MySQLshared**–These are the libraries that are shared with the MySQL client.
- **MySQL devel** – These are header files and libraries which are widely used during the compilation of other programs using MySQL.
- **MySQL client** – These programs allow development of a connection to the server and further interactions with it.

In order to continue with your setup, you must follow the instructions below:

1. Use the root user to log into the system.
2. Change to the RPM-containing directory.

3. Execute the command below to install the MySQL database server. Keep in mind to substitute "the filename in italics with a desired file name of your RPM."

[root@host] # rpm -i MySQL-6.0.12-0.i395.rpm

This function is responsible for the installation of the MySQL server and for creation of its user, the required setup and automated startup of the MySQL server.

All MySQL associated binaries can be easily located in the /usr / bin as well as the /usr / sbin directories. Every database and table would be generated in the /var / lib / mysql directory.

The commands below are optional and can be used to install the other RPMs using the same approach, but it is highly recommended to install all these RPMs on your system:

[root@host]# rpm -i MySQL-client-6.0.12-0.i395.rpm
[root@host]# rpm -i MySQL-devel-6.0.12-0.i395.rpm
[root@host]# rpm -i MySQL-shared-6.0.12-0.i395.rpm
[root@host]# rpm -i MySQL-bench-6.0.12-0.i395.rpm

Installation of MySQL on Windows Operating System

To install MySQL on any version of Windows is much easier now than in the past, as MySQL is now offered as an installation package. All you have to do is save the installer package on your system, open the zipped file then execute the setup.

Installation processes in the default setup.exe file is insignificant and all of them are installed under C:\mysql by default.

To test the server for the first time simply open user interface using the command prompt. Go to the MySQL server location that is likely going to be C:\mysql\bin then enter these keywords: mysqldexe console.

After successful installation some startup and InnoDB messages will be displayed on your screen. A failed installation may be related to system permissions issue. It is important to ensure that the directory holding the data is available to every user (likely MySQL) under which the procedures of the database are run.

MySQL cannot be added to the start menu with installation and no user-friendly way is offered to exit the server. So, you should consider stopping the process manually with the use of mysql admin, task manager and list, or other methods specified for Windows, instead of double-clicking on the mysqld executable to launch the server.

Installing MySQL on Macintosh Operating System

Follow the instruction below for installation of MySQL on Mac OS X:

- ➢ Download the disk image file (.dmg) containing the MySQL package installer. For mounting the disk image and viewing the contents, click twice on the .dmg file.
- ➢ Now, click twice on the MySQL installer package. The name of the OS X MySQL installer package version would be in accordance with the MySQL as well as your computer's current OS X version. For instance, if you could download the package for MySQL 6.1.46 and OS X 11.2, then double click on the mysql 6.1.22-osx-11.2-x90 64.pkg.
- ➢ The opening installer message will be displayed on the screen. To start installation, click Continue.

- The accompanying GNU General Public License will be displayed for all downloads of the MySQL community version. Click Continue and then Agree to proceed.
- You can select Install to run the installation wizard from the Installation Type page with all default settings. Then click Customize to select the components you desire to install Launchd Support or Preference Pane and MySQL server all of which will be activated by default.
- To start the installation process, click Install.
- After successful installation has been done, an Install Succeeded message with a brief overview will be displayed on the screen. You can exit the installation assistant at this point and start using the MySQL server.

MySQL has been configured now but cannot be launched automatically. You can either select launchctlor, click on Start on the Preference Pane to fire up the MySQL server.

Installations done using the package installer will configure the files within /usr / local directory, that matches the name of the installation version and operating system being used. For instance, the installer file mysql 6.1.22-osx-11.2-x90 64.dmg installs MySQL into /usr/local/mysql 6.1.22-osx-11.2-x90 64/. A symbolic connection to a particular directory depending on the version or platform will be generated during the setup phase from /usr / local / mysql, which is automatically updated while you are installing the package. The table below illustrates the installation directory layouts.

Directory	Contents of Directory
bin, scripts	Includes server and programs for utility and client
data	Includes log file and database
docs	Includes help documents such as Release Notes
include	Includes header file
lib	Library
man	Includes manual page for Unix
mysql-test	Includes test cases for MySQL
share	Includes various support files such as errors, file samples for configuration used to install the database
sql-bench	Includes various benchmark
support-files	Includes file samples for configuration and

Directory	Contents of Directory
	scripts
/tmp/mysql.sock	Includes the location of the MySQL Unix socket

Creating a New Database Using MySQL Server

In MySQL server, databases are implemented as directories that contain all the files corresponding to the tables in a particular database.

Now that you have installed the MySQL Server, you can follow the instructions below to generate new databases with the CREATE command, using the syntax below:

CREATE DATABASE [IF NOT EXISTS] db_title
[CHARACTER SET chrst_title]
[COLLATE collatn_title]

In the syntax above, the first step is specifying the database_name right after the CREATE DATABASE command. In the MySQL server instance, the title of any database being created must be unique. When you're trying to build a database with an existing name, the server will abort the action. Next you can indicate the choice IF NOT EXISTS to prevent an infringement, if you erroneously generate a new database that shares its name with a database that already exists on the server. In this scenario, MySQL will not generate an issue but will instead terminate the CREATE DATABASE statement. Lastly, when the new database is created, you are able to indicate the character set and combination requirements. If the clauses CHARACTER SET and COLLATE are omitted, then MySQL utilizes the default settings for the new database.

Alternatively, you can build a new database using **MySQL Workbench** and following the steps below:

1. Open MySQL Workbench then select the set up new Connection icon on the screen.
2. Enter desired title for your connection and click on the Test Connection icon. A windowpane requiring the root user password would be displayed in MySQL Workbench. You are required to enter the root user password, click on the checkbox for the save password option and select OK.
3. For connecting with the MySQL server, click twice on the connection name Local. MySQL Workbench opens the window containing four different components namely: Query, Navigator, Info and O/P.

4. Select the icon to create a new schema on the screen. The database is also known as schema in MySQL. Therefore, developing a new schema just implies that you are generating a new database.

5. In the subsequent window you are required to provide the schema name and modify the collation and character set as required then select the Apply icon.

6. The software will open up in a new window displaying the SQL script that needs to be executed. Keep in mind that the CREATE SCHEMA query will lead to the same result as the CREATE DATABASE query. If all goes well, the new database will be generated and displayed in the "schemas tab of the Navigator section."

7. For selection of the testdb database, simply right click on its name and select Set as Default Schema.

8. The testdb node would be open so you can run queries on testdb using the MySQL Workbench.

Managing a Database Using MySQL Server

Once all the databases containing your desired data have been created, you can selectively display and use the content needed using the instructions below.

Display Databases

The SHOW DATABASES statement is utilized to list all the databases currently existing on the MySQL server. You can inspect only your database or every database on the server through the use of a SHOW DATABASES statement before building a new database. For example, if you assume that the databases, we have created so far are all on the MySQL Server and the *SHOW DATABASES;* statement is executed, you will see the result as information_schema; *database_baseball; database_HealthPlus; mysql.*

Now you know that there are four different databases on your MySQL server. The information_schema and mysql are default databases that are created upon installation of the MySQL server and the other two databases, namely *database_baseball* and *database_HealthPlus* were created by us.

Selection of a Database

Before operating with a specific database, you are required to first inform MySQL, which database you would like to operate by utilizing the USE command as below:

USE db_nam;

To select the *database_HealthPlus, you can write the command as below:*

USE database_HealthPlus;

Creating a NewDatabaseTableUsing MySQL Server

You will be using the CREATE TABLE statement to build new tables. The CREATE TABLE command is considered as one of the most complicated statements in SQL. A simple CREATE TABLE syntax can be written as below:

CREATE TABLE [IF NOT EXISTS] tbl_nam(
colum_lst
) ENGINE = storag_engin

Start by indicating the table name after the CREATE TABLE clause, that you would like to create. The name of the new table must be unique. The IF NOT EXISTS is one of the auxiliary clauses that allow for verification of whether the table being build has previously been created in that database. If there is a duplication in the table name, the entire statement will be ignored by MySQL and the new table will not be generated. You are advised to use this clause in every statement for creating tables, in order to prevent an accidental creation of any new table name that can be found on the server.

Next, in the column list section, a list of table columns can be specified, and each column name can be distinguished with the use of commas.

Lastly, in the ENGINE clause, you have the option to indicate the table storage engine. Any storage engine like InnoDB and MyISAM could be used. If the storage engine is not specifically declared, MySQL will be using the default InnoDB engine.

The following syntax can be utilized to describe a table column in the CREATE TABLE statement:

column_ namdata_ typ(length) [NOT NULL] [DEFAULT val] [AUTO_INCREMENT]

In the syntax above, the column name has been specified by the column_name clause. Each column contains a particular type and the desired length of the data, for example, VARCHAR(255). The NOT NULL clause indicates that NULL value will not be permitted by this column.

The value DEFAULT can be utilized to indicate the default value for specific columns. The AUTO_INCREMENT shows that when adding any new rows, the column value would be automatically created by the column. The AUTO_INCREMENT columns in each table are unique. For instance, you will be able to build a new table to store data pertaining to tasks called "tsks", with the command below:

```
CREATE TABLE IF NOT EXISTS tsks (
    tsk_id INT AUTO_INCREMENT,
    titlVARCHAR(255) NOT NULL,
    strt_dte DATE,
    due_dte DATE,
    stats TINYINT NOT NULL,
    prity TINYINT NOT NULL,
    desc TEXT,
    PRIMARY KEY (tsk_id)
) ENGINE=INNODB;
```

In the syntax above, the tsk Id is an auto increment column. In case the INSERT query is used for adding a new record to the table, with the tsk Id column value not being specified, the tsk Id column will be given an auto-generated integer value starting with '1'. The tsk Id column has been specified as the primary key.

The title column has been given a variable character string data type with max allowed length of 255 characters. This implies that a string of characters larger than 255 characters in length cannot be inserted in this column. The NOT NULL suggests that a value is required for the column i.e. when inserting or updating this column, a value must be provided.

The strtdte and due dte are date columns that will allow NULL values.

The stats and prity are the "TINYINT" columns and will not permit NULL values.

The desc column is a TEXT column that will allow NULL values.

Inserting Data into a Table on the MySQL Server

To add single or multiple records into the table, the "INSERT" statement is used, as shown in the syntax below:

INSERT INTO tbl(p1,p2,...)
VALUES (q1,q2,...);

In the statement above, the table name must be specified next to a list of desired columns separated by "commas" written within "parentheses," following the INSERT INTO clause. After which, all the values separated by commas pertaining to the columns within the parentheses must be written, following the VALUES function. Make sure there is same quantity of columns and corresponding column values. Furthermore, the column positions must correspond with the position of the column values.

Execute the code below to add one or more records to the table, using only one INSERT statement:

INSERT INTO tbl (p1, p2,...)
VALUES
  (q11, q12,...),
  (q21, q22,...),
  ...
  (qmm, qm2,...);"

The example below will generate three rows or records in the table "tutorials tbl" and display the confirmation that the "row has been affected":

root@host# mysql -u root -p password;
Entrpswd: *****

msql> using BOOK;

Db changes

msql> INSERT INTO book_tble

   ->(book_titl, bookl_athr, submsn_dat)

   ->VALUES

   ->('Master the Code', 'Pam Podds', NOW());

Qry OK, 1 rwaffctd (0.02 secs)

msql> INSERT INTO book_tble

   ->(book_titl, bookl_athr, submsn_dat)

   ->VALUES

   ->('Master the Code', 'Bob Suddds, NOW());

Qry OK, 1 rwaffctd (0.02 secs)

mysql> INSERT INTO book_tble

   ->(book_titl, bookl_athr, submsn_dat)

   ->VALUES

   ->('Skills of a Programmer', 'Samuel Jack', '2017-15-09');

Qry OK, 1 rwaffctd (0.02 secs)

msql>"

Here is another example, the query below can be utilized for inserting a new record to the tsks table that was created earlier:

"INSERT INTO

tsks(titl,prity)

VALUES

('Learning all the coding languages, 2);

1 row(s) affected;"

The output should look like the sample image below with the column and row values used in the code above:

task_id	title	start_date	due_date	priority	description
1	Learn MySQL INSERT Statement	NULL	NULL	1	NULL

We indicated the values, in the example above, only for the title and priority columns. MySQL will use the default values for the other non-specified columns.

The tsk_id column has been specified as an auto increment column. This implies that upon insertion of a new record to the table, MySQL will generate a subsequent integer.

The strt_dte, due_dte and desc columns have been specified to hold NULL as the default value, so if no values are specified in the INSERT statement, MySQL will insert NULL into those columns.

To add default values into desired columns, either simply disregard the column name and its corresponding values or indicate the name of the columns in the INSERT INTO function and type DEFAULT in the VALUES clause. For example, in the syntax below the prity column has been specified with the DEFAULT keyword.

INSERT INTO
tsks(titl,prity)
VALUES
('Learning how to use various functions for coding',
DEFAULT);

You can insert dates into the table using the YYYY-MM-DD format, which represents year, month and date in the mentioned order. For example, you can add the strtdte and due date values to the tsks table using the command below:

INSERT INTO tsks (titl, strt_dte, due_dte)
VALUES ('Learning how to use date function for coding','2019-02-19','2019-12-18'):

The VALUES clause also supports expressions as shown in the example below, where the syntax will add a new task utilizing the current date for strtdte and due dte columns using the CURRENT_DATE() function. Remember the CURRENT_DATE() function will always return the current date in the system.

"INSERT INTO tsks(titl,strt_dte,due_dte)
VALUES
('Learning how to use variousfunctions for
coding',CURRENT_DATE(),CURRENT_DATE());

To insert multiple rows or records in the, take a look at the example below of the tsks table, where each record is indicated as values listed in the VALUES clause:

INSERT INTO tsks (titl, prity)
VALUES
('This is how we start', 2),
('Moving to the next task', 3),
('Moving to the next task', 4),
('Moving to the final task before the weekend', 5);

The resulting output should be:*4 row(s) affected Records:4 Dupes: 0 Warning: 0*, which implies that the records were added to the table and there are no duplicates or warnings in the table.

Creating a Temporary table in the database using MySQL server

A temp table in MySQL is a peculiar kind of table that enables the storage of a temporary outcome set for reuse over multiple times over the same session.

A temp table is extremely useful when querying information that needs only one SELECT statement containing the JOIN clause, which is not feasible or costly. In such a scenario, the temporary table can be used as a storage for the immediate result which can be processed further using a different query.

A temp table in MySQL may have the characteristics listed below:

- A temp table is generated by executing the CREATE TEMPORARY TABLE statement. Note that between CREATE and TABLE functions, the TEMPORARY keyword must be added.
- When the session is completed or the connection is ended, MySQL server will automatically remove the temporary table from its memory. Another thing to remember is that once you are done with the temporary table, it can be explicitly deleted utilizing the DROP TABLE command.
- Only the user that generates the temp table is able to access it. Other users can potentially generate multiple temporary tables with the same name and still not cause

any error since they can only be seen by the user who produced that specific temporary table. Two or more temporary tables cannot, however, share the same name over the same session.

- In a database, a temporary table may be given the same name as a standard table. The existing employee table, for instance, cannot be accessed by creating a temporary table called employees, within the sample database. All queries you execute on the employees table will now be referred to the temporary employees table. When the employees temporary table is deleted, the permanent employees table would still be in the system and can be accessed again.

While it can be given the same title as a standard table without triggering any error, it is advised to have a different name for the temp table. As the same name can lead to confusion and may result in an unexpected loss of information. For example, you cannot distinguish between these two types of tables, if the connection to the database server is dismissed for some reason and then automatically reconnected to the server. Then, rather than the temp table, you could enter a DROP TABLE statement to delete the standard table unexpectedly.

Now, a temp table can be created in MySQL by using the "TEMPORARY" keyword within statements used to generate new tables. For instance, the command below will generate a temp table containing only the top ten clients by profit with the given table name as "top10clients":

```
CREATE TEMPORARY TABLE top10clients
SELECT x.clientNbr,
y.clientNam,
    ROUND(SUM(z.amt), 2) sale
FROM pay a
INNER JOIN clients y ON y.clientNbr = a.clientNbr
GROUP BY a.clientNbr
ORDER BY sale DESC
LIMIT 10;
```

Using this temp table, you can further run queries on this table like you would on a standard or permanent table in the database.

```
SELECT
clientNbr,
clientNam,
  sale
FROM
  top10clients
```

ORDER BY sale;

Creating a NewTable from an Existing Table in the DatabaseUsing MySQL Server

You may also generate a copy of a table that can be found in the table with the use of the CREATE TABLE command, as shown in the syntax below:

CREATE TABLE nw_tbl_nam AS
 SELECT col1, col2,...
 FROM existin_tbl_nam
 WHERE ....;"

The new table will have the same specifications for the columns as the parent table. It is possible to select all columns
or a particular column. If a new table is generated using a table that already exists in the database, then the current values from the parent table will be automatically loaded into the new table. For example, in the syntax below a table called TstTbl will be created as a replica of the parent Clients table:

CREATE TABLE TstTbl AS
SELECT clientnam, contctnam
FROM clients;

You might encounter a scenario, when you require a precise copy or clone of a table and the standard statement for creation of new tables does not meet the requirement, since you would like the clone to contain the identical indexes, default values, etc as the parent table.

This scenario can be addressed by executing the measures provided below:

- The "SHOW CREATE TABLE" can be used to execute a CREATE TABLE query specifying the structures, index and other feature of the source or parent table.
- Adjust the query to alter the table name to be same as the clone table and run the query. You would be able to get the precise clone of the table with this method.
- Optionally, if you would also like to copy the table contents, you can execute an INSERT INTO... SELECT statement.

For example, you can generate a clone table for tution_tab using the syntax below:

FIRST, copy the entire schema of the table:

msql> SHOW CREATE TABLE tution_tab \G;

Table: tution_tab

Creating Tab: CREATE TABLE 'tution_tab' (

  `tution_id ` *int (15) NOT NULL auto_increment,*

  `tution_titl ` *varchar (100) NOT NULL default',*

  `tution_author' varchar (40) NOT NULL default',*

  `submsn_dte' dte default NULL,*

  PRIMARY KEY (`tution_id `),

  UNIQUE KEY 'AUTHOR_INDEX' (`tution_author')

) *TYPE = MyISAM*

2 rows in set (0.02 secs)

ERROR:

"No query specified"

SECOND, change the name of the parent table to generate a new clone table:

msql> CREATE TABLE clone_tbl (

-> `tution_id ` *int (15) NOT NULL auto_increment,*

-> `tution_titl ` *varchar (100) NOT NULL default',*

-> `tution_author' varchar (40) NOT NULL default',*

-> `submsn_dte' dte default NULL,*

-> *PRIMARY KEY (* `tution_id `),

->*UNIQUE KEY 'AUTHOR_INDEX' (* `tution_author')

) *TYPE = MyISAM*

Query OK, 1 row affected (0.02 secs)

LASTLY, if you need to replicate the source table to the clone tables, you can use the command below:

msql> INSERT INTO clone_tbl (tutorial_id,
  ->tutorial_title,
  ->tutorial_author,
  ->submission_date)

  -> SELECT tutorial_id,tutorial_title,
  ->tutorial_author,submission_date
  -> FROM tutorials_tbl;
Query OK, 3 rows affected (0.07 sec)
Records: 3 Duplicates: 0 Warnings: 0"

DERVIVED TABLES in MySQL Server

A derived table can be defined as virtual table obtained upon execution of a SELECT statements. It is comparable to temp tables, however, in the SELECT statement it is much easier and quicker to use a derived table than a temp table as it would not entail additional steps to create the temp table.

There is often interchangeable use of the term derived table and subquery. When the FROM clause of a SELECT query uses a stand-alone subquery, it is called as a derived table. For example, the syntax below can be used to create a derived table:

SELECT
col_list
FROM
  (SELECT
col_list
  FROM
    tab_1) dervd_tab_nam;
WHERE dervd_tab_nam.d1 > 1;

A derived table is required to have an alias, which can be referenced in future queries, however, there is no such requirement for a subquery. If there is no alias defined for a derived table, the error message below will be displayed by MySQL:

"Every derived table must have its own alias"

Review the example below of a query that will generate Top six products by sales in 2013 from the order and order detail tables in the MySQL server "sample database":

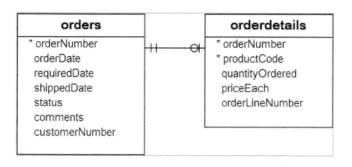

SELECT

pdctCode,

   ROUND(SUM(qtyOrdrd * pricEch)) sale

FROM

orderdetail

     INNER JOIN

   order USING (orderNo)

WHERE

YEAR(shippdDte) = 2013

GROUP BY pdctCode

ORDER BY sale DESC

LIMIT 6;

The resulting table would be similar to the picture shown below:

productCode	sales
S18_3232	103480
S10_1949	67985
S12_1108	59852
S12_3891	57403
S12_1099	56462

The resulting derived table shown in the picture above can be joined with the product table using the syntax below:

products

* productCode
productName
productLine
productScale
productVendor
productDescription
quantityInStock
buyPrice
MSRP

SELECT

pdctNam, sale

FROM

(SELECT

pdctCode,

ROUND(SUM(qtyOrdrd * pricEch)) sale

FROM

orderdetail

INNER JOIN order USING (orderNo)

WHERE

YEAR(shippdDte) = 2013

GROUP BY pdctCode

ORDER BY sale DESC

LIMIT 6) top6products2013

INNER JOIN

product USING (pdctCode);"

The query above will result in the output similar to the one shown in the picture below:

productName	sales
▶ 1992 Ferrari 360 Spider red	103480
1952 Alpine Renault 1300	67985
2001 Ferrari Enzo	59852
1969 Ford Falcon	57403
1968 Ford Mustang	56462

To drive this concept home, review a relatively complicated example of derived tables below:

Assume that the clients from the year 2019 have to be classified into three groups: platinum, gold and silver. Moreover, taking into consideration the criteria below, you would like to calculate the number of clients within each group:

- Platinum clients with orders larger than 99K in quantity.
- Gold clients with quantity orders ranging from 9K to 99K.
- Silver clients with orders less than 9K in quantity.

To generate a query for this analysis, you must first classify each client into appropriate group using CASE clause and GROUP BY function as shown in the syntax below:

SELECT
clientNo,
   *ROUND(SUM(qtyOrdrd * pricEch)) sale,*
   (CASE
     *WHEN SUM(qtyOrdrd * pricEch) < 9000 THEN 'Silver'*
     *WHEN SUM(qtyOrdrd * pricEch) BETWEEN 9000 AND 99000 THEN 'Gold'*
     *WHEN SUM(qtyOrdrd * pricEch) >99000 THEN 'Platinum'*
   END) clientGroup
FROM
orderdetail
   INNER JOIN
   orders USING (orderNo)
WHERE
YEAR(shippdDte) = 2019

GROUP BY clientNo;

The query output will be similar to the one shown in the picture below:

customerNumber	sales	customerGroup
103	14571	Gold
112	32642	Gold
114	53429	Gold
121	51710	Gold
124	167783	Platinum
128	34651	Gold
129	40462	Gold
131	22293	Gold
141	189840	Platinum

Now, you can execute the code below to generate a derived table and group the clients as needed:

SELECT
clientGroup,
COUNT(cg.clientGroup) AS grpCount
FROM
  (SELECT
clientNo,
     ROUND(SUM(qtyOrdrd * pricEch)) sales,
     (CASE

*WHEN SUM(qtyOrdrd * pricEch) <9000 THEN
'Silver'*

*WHEN SUM(qtyOrdrd * pricEch) BETWEEN 9000
AND 99000 THEN 'Gold'*

*WHEN SUM(qtyOrdrd * pricEch) >99000 THEN
'Platinum'*

END) clientGroup

FROM

orderdetail

INNER JOIN orders USING (orderNo)

WHERE

YEAR(shippdDte) = 2019

GROUP BY clientNo) cg

GROUP BY cg.clientGroup; "

The query output will be similar to the one shown in the picture below:

customerGroup	groupCount
Gold	61
Silver	8
Platinum	4

Chapter 3:Advanced SQL Functions

The most common command used in SQL is the SELECT command, which we have already used in the exercises mentioned earlier in this book. So, now let me give you a deep dive into the SQL SELECT command and various clauses that can be used with it.

MySQL SELECT

You can selectively fetch desired data from tables or views, using the SELECT statement. As you already know, similar to a spreadsheet, a table comprises rows and columns. You are highly likely to view a subset of columns, a subset of rows, or a combo of them both. The outcome of this query is known as a "result set," which are lists of records comprising the same number of columns per record.

In the picture shown below of the employee table from the "MySQL sample database", the table has 8 different columns and several records, as shown in the picture below:

employeeNumb	lastName	firstName	extension	email	officeCode	reportsTo	jobTitle
1002	Murphy	Diane	x5800	dmurphy@classicmodelcars.com	1	NULL	President
1056	Patterson	Mary	x4611	mpatterso@classicmodelcars.com	1	1002	VP Sales
1076	Firrelli	Jeff	x9273	jfirrelli@classicmodelcars.com	1	1002	VP Marketing
1088	Patterson	William	x4871	wpatterson@classicmodelcars.com	6	1056	Sales Manager (APAC)
1102	Bondur	Gerard	x5408	gbondur@classicmodelcars.com	4	1056	Sale Manager (EMEA)
1143	Bow	Anthony	x5428	abow@classicmodelcars.com	1	1056	Sales Manager (NA)
1165	Jennings	Leslie	x3291	ljennings@classicmodelcars.com	1	1143	Sales Rep
1166	Thompson	Leslie	x4065	lthompson@classicmodelcars.com	1	1143	Sales Rep
1188	Firrelli	Julie	x2173	jfirrelli@classicmodelcars.com	2	1143	Sales Rep
1216	Patterson	Steve	x4334	spatterson@classicmodelcars.com	2	1143	Sales Rep
1286	Tseng	Foon Yue	x2248	ftseng@classicmodelcars.com	3	1143	Sales Rep
1323	Vanauf	George	x4102	gvanauf@classicmodelcars.com	3	1143	Sales Rep
1337	Bondur	Loui	x6493	lbondur@classicmodelcars.com	4	1102	Sales Rep
1370	Hernandez	Gerard	x2028	ghernande@classicmodelcars.com	4	1102	Sales Rep
1401	Castillo	Pamela	x2759	pcastillo@classicmodelcars.com	4	1102	Sales Rep
1501	Bott	Larry	x2311	lbott@classicmodelcars.com	7	1102	Sales Rep

The SELECT query dictates the columns and records that can be fetched from the table. For instance, if you would like to display just the fstnam, lstnam, and job titl of all the employees or you selectively desire to see the info pertaining to employees with job titl as sales reps, then you will be able to utilize the SELECT query to achieve this.

Here is a standard syntax for SELECT statement:

SELECT
    col_1, col_2, ...
FROM
    tab_1
[INNER | LEFT |RIGHT] JOIN tab_2 ON condition
WHERE

96

condition
GROUP BY col_1
HAVING grp_condition
ORDER BY col_1
LIMIT offst, len;

The SELECT query above contains various provisions, as described below:

- The SELECT clause after a list of columns isolated by asterisks or commas suggests that all columns are to be returned.
- The FROM clause defines the table or view from which the data should be queried.
- The JOIN clause receives associated data from other tables as dictated by the specified join criteria.
- In the output, the WHERE clause will be utilized for selectively filtering the rows or records.
- The GROUP BY clause will be utilized to selectively group a set of records and apply aggregate functions to each group.
- The HAVING clause will be utilized to sift through a group on the basis of the GROUP BY clause specified groups.
- The ORDER BY clause can be utilized for specifying a list of columns to be sorted.

- The LIMIT clause is utilized for restricting the number of records displayed upon execution of the command.

Note that only SELECT and FROM clauses are necessary to execute the command and all other clauses can be used on ad-hoc basis.

For example, in case you would like to selectively display certain records of all employees, you can utilize the syntax below:

SELECT
lstnam, fstnam, jobtitl
FROM
  employee;

But if you would like to view all the columns in this table, use the syntax below:

*SELECT * FROM employee;*

In practice, it is recommended to list the columns you would like to view instead of using the asterisk (*) command, as the asterisk (*) will return all column data, some of which you may not be allowed to use. It will create network traffic and non-essential input output disk between the server and the app. If the columns are defined explicitly, then the result set becomes simpler to predict and handle. Suppose you are using the asterisk(*) and some other user modified the table and generated additional columns, you would receive a result set containing different columns than needed. Moreover, the use of asterisk(*) can potentially reveal sensitive data to unauthorized users.

MySQL SELECT DISTINCT

You can receive duplicate rows when searching for information from a table. You could utilize the DISTINCT clause in the SELECT query to get rid of these redundant rows.

The DISTINCT clause syntax is given below:

SELECT DISTINCT
  cols
FROM
tab_nam
WHERE
whr_condtns;

EXAMPLE

The syntax below presents an example for the DISTINCT clause, used to selectively view unique records of the column lstnam from the employee table.

First, all the records from the column lstnam from the employee tables must be displayed using the syntax below:

SELECT
lstnam
FROM
  employee
ORDER BY lstnam;

Now to get rid of the repeated last names, use the syntax below:

SELECT DISTINCT
lstnam
FROM
  employee
ORDER BY lstnam;

Please note, if a column has been indicated to hold NULL values and the DISTINCT clause is used. Only one NULL value will be retained by the sever since the DISTINCT clause will consider all NULL values as identical.

Using DISTINCTClause on MultipleColumns

To accomplish this MySQL server will use a combination of all values in selected columns to identify unique records in the result set. For example, you can view singular combinations of cty and stat columns from the clients table using the syntax below:

SELECT DISTINCT
  stat, cty
FROM
clients
WHERE
  stat IS NOT NULL
ORDER BY stat, cty;

MySQL ORDER BY

When using SELECT statements, the output will not be organized in a particular format. That is where the ORDER BY clause can be utilized to organize the output as desired. The ORDER BY clause would allow sifting through the output on the basis of one or more columns as well as sorting a number of columns in increasing or decreasing order.

Here is the ORDER BY clause syntax:

SELECT col01, col02,...
FROM tbl
ORDER BY col01 [ASC|DESC], col02 [ASC|DESC], ...;

As you would expect the ASC means ascending and the DESC means descending. By default, if ASC or DESC has not been specified explicitly, the ORDER BY clause can sort the output in ascending order.

EXAMPLE

The syntax below presents an example for the ORDER BY clause, used to selectively view contacts from the clients table and sort them in ascending order of the column lstnam.

SELECT
contctlstnam,
contctfstnam
FROM
clients
ORDER BY

contctlstnam;

A sample of the ascending result set is shown in the picture below:

contactLastname	contactFirstname
Accorti	Paolo
Altagar,G M	Raanan
Andersen	Mel
Anton	Carmen
Ashworth	Rachel
Barajas	Miguel
Benitez	Violeta
Bennett	Helen
Berglund	Christina

Now, if you wanted to view the last name in descending order, you will use the syntax below:

SELECT
contctlstnam,
contctfstnam
FROM
clients
ORDER BY
contctlstnam DESC;"

A sample of the descending result set is shown in the picture below:

	contactLastname	contactFirstname
▶	Young	Jeff
	Young	Julie
	Young	Mary
	Young	Dorothy
	Yoshido	Juri
	Walker	Brydey
	Victorino	Wendy
	Urs	Braun
	Tseng	Jerry

Or, if you would like to arrange the column lstnamin decreasing order and the fstnam in the increasing order, you can utilize the ASC and DESC clause in the same query but with the relevant column as shown in the syntax below:

SELECT
Contctlstnam,
contctfstnam
FROM
clients
ORDER BY
contctlstnam DESC,

contctfstnam ASC;

A sample of the result set is shown in the picture below, where the ORDER BY clause will first sort the lst name in decreasing order and then subsequently sort the fstnam in the increasing order:

contactLastname	contactFirstname
Young	Dorothy
Young	Jeff
Young	Julie
Young	Mary
Yoshido	Juri
Walker	Brydey
Victorino	Wendy
Urs	Braun
Tseng	Jerry

MySQL WHERE

The WHERE clause enables the search criteria to be specified for the records displayed after running the query.

The WHERE clause syntax is given below:

SELECT
slct_lst

FROM

tab_nam

WHERE

srch_cndtn;"

The "search_condition" is a composite of single or multiple predicate utilizing the logical operators, as shown in the table below. A "predicate" in SQL, can be defined as a query that assesses unknown, false or true.

Operators	Descriptions
=	Equals. Can be used with any type of data
<>or !=	Not equals
<	Less than. Mostly used with numeric and date data type
>	Greater than
<=	Less than or equals
>=	Greater than or equals

The final result set includes any record from the tab_nam that makes the "search_condition" to be evaluated as valid.

In addition to the SELECT statement, you may indicate the rows that need to be updated and deleted, utilizing the WHERE clause in the DELETE and UPDATE query.

EXAMPLE

The syntax below presents an example for the WHERE clause, used to selectively view employees with job title as Sales Reps from the employee table:

SELECT
lstnam,
fstnam,
jobtitl
FROM
  employee
WHERE
jobtitl = 'Sales Reps';

Although the WHERE clause is usually defined at the very end, MySQL query first selects the corresponding rows after evaluating the phrase in the WHERE clause. It selects the rows with a job title as Sales Reps followed by the selection of

the column in the SELECT clause from the select list. The
highlighted rows in the picture below, include the final result set
columns and rows.

employeeNumber	lastName	firstName	extension	email	officeCode	reportsTo	jobTitle
1002	Murphy	Diane	x5800	dmurphy@classicmodelcars.com	1	NULL	President
1056	Patterson	Mary	x4611	mpatterson@classicmodelcars.com	1	1002	VP Sales
1076	Firrelli	Jeff	x9273	jfirrelli@classicmodelcars.com	1	1002	VP Marketing
1088	Patterson	William	x4871	wpatterson@classicmodelcars.com	6	1056	Sales Manager (APAC)
1102	Bondur	Gerard	x5408	gbondur@classicmodelcars.com	4	1056	Sale Manager (EMEA)
1143	Bow	Anthony	x5428	abow@classicmodelcars.com	1	1056	Sales Manager (NA)
1165	Jennings	Leslie	x3291	ljennings@classicmodelcars.com	1	1143	Sales Rep
1165	Thompson	Leslie	x4065	lthompson@classicmodelcars.com	1	1143	Sales Rep
1188	Firrelli	Julie	x2173	jfirrelli@classicmodelcars.com	2	1143	Sales Rep
1216	Patterson	Steve	x4334	spatterson@classicmodelcars.com	2	1143	Sales Rep
1286	Tseng	Foon Yue	x2248	ftseng@classicmodelcars.com	3	1143	Sales Rep
1323	Vanauf	George	x4102	gvanauf@classicmodelcars.com	3	1143	Sales Rep
1337	Bondur	Loui	x6493	lbondur@classicmodelcars.com	4	1102	Sales Rep
1370	Hernandez	Gerard	x2028	ghernande@classicmodelcars.com	4	1102	Sales Rep

MySQL JOIN Statements

The MySQL JOIN function is a way to link information between
one or more tables on the basis of common attributes or column
values between the selected tables. A relational database
comprises of various tables that have been linked by a shared or
common column, known as foreign key. As a result,
information in each individual table can be deemed
incomplete from the business perspective. For instance, there
are two separate tables in the MySQL sample database called
order and order detail that have been connected to each other
using a column called orderNo. You will have to search for
information in both the order and the order detail table to
obtain complete order information.

There are 6 different SQL JOINS functions, namely, "INNER JOIN,""LEFT JOIN," "RIGHT JOIN,""CROSS JOIN" and "SELF JOIN."

We will be using tables named to1 and to2 as described in the syntax below, in order to facilitate your understanding of each type of JOIN. The pattern column in both to1 and to2 tables serves as the common column between them.

CREATE TABLE to1 (
  id INT PRIMARY KEY,
ptrn VARCHAR(45) NOT NULL
);

CREATE TABLE to2 (
  id VARCHAR(45) PRIMARY KEY,
ptrn VARCHAR(45) NOT NULL
);

We can insert some data into the two tables using INSERT function as shown in the syntax below:

INSERT INTO to1(id, ptrn)
VALUES(01,'Pivots'),
  (02,'Bricks'),

(03,'Grids');

INSERT INTO to2(id, ptrn)
VALUES('X','Bricks'),
   ('Y','Grids'),
   ('Z','Diamonds');"

The result of the syntax above will be similar to the one shown in the picture below:

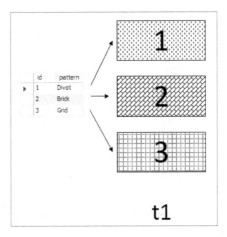

Now, let us look at every type of "JOIN" clause in detail!

"INNER JOIN"

The MySQL INNER JOIN is used to align records of a table with another, so that rows containing columns from the two tables can be queried.

The SELECT statement is not required to contain the INNER JOIN clause for execution, which appears right next to the FROM clause.

You must indicate the following requirements before using the INNER JOIN clause:

- Start with the primary table to be included in the FROM clause.
- Then, choose the table that needs to be connected to the primary table included in the INNER JOIN clause, in step 1. Remember theoretically you can join one table to multiple tables at the same time. However, it is recommended to restrict the number of tables to be joined, to achieve higher performance and efficiency.
- Lastly, the join condition or join predicate must be defined. Following the initial "ON" keyword the join condition can be indicated. The join condition is the rule that dictates the matching of a record in the main table with the rows from another.

The INNER JOIN syntax is given below:

SELECT col_lst
FROM to1
INNER JOIN to2 ON join_cndtn1
INNER JOIN to3 ON join_cndtn2

...

WHERE whr_cndtns;

Now, for further simplification of the query above, just assume that you are interested in linking only tables to1 and to2 using the syntax below:

SELECT col_lst
FROM to1
INNER JOIN to2 ON jn_cndtn;

This clause will compare every row ofto1 with every single row of to2 to determine whether the two tables fulfill the defined condition. Once the condition has been satisfied, a new record will be returned, consisting of columns from both to1 and to2.

Note that the records in both to1 and to2 need to be merged according to the conditions. If none of the records from the two tables are identified meeting the join condition, an empty result set is returned by the query. The same logic applies when more than two tables are joined.

The Venn diagram below shows the working of the "INNER JOIN" clause. The records in the output are required to be present in both to1 and to2 as represented by the section overlapping the 2 circles, depicting each table respectively.

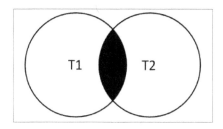

EXAMPLE

Consider the two tables from the "sample database," shown in the picture below. The second table is connected to the first table by referencing the productline column. Therefore, the productline column serves as foreign key in the products table.

Conventionally, tables that have foreign key relationships are queried using the JOIN clause.

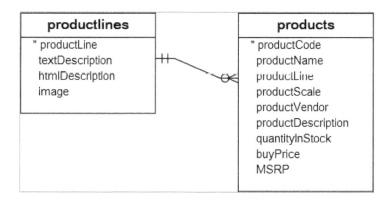

Let's assume that you would like to view the pdctCod and pdctNam columns from the second table as well as txtDesc of the product lined from the first table. You can accomplish this by using the syntax below and matching the rows of both the tables on the basis of productline columns in the two tables.

SELECT
pdctCod,
pdctNam,
txtDesc
FROM
pdcts to1
    INNER JOIN
pdctlines to2 ON to1.pductlin = to2.pductlin;
A sample of the result set is shown in the picture below:

productCode	productName	textDescription
S10_1949	1952 Alpine Renault 1300	Attention car enthusiasts: Make your wildest car ownership dreams come true.
S10_4757	1972 Alfa Romeo GTA	Attention car enthusiasts: Make your wildest car ownership dreams come true.
S10_4962	1962 LanciaA Delta 16V	Attention car enthusiasts: Make your wildest car ownership dreams come true.
S12_1099	1968 Ford Mustang	Attention car enthusiasts: Make your wildest car ownership dreams come true.
S12_1108	2001 Ferrari Enzo	Attention car enthusiasts: Make your wildest car ownership dreams come true.

Here's a tip!

Since both the tables contain identical column called "productline", you could use the simpler query below (without the need of using the table aliases) and obtain the same "result set" as shown in the picture above:

SELECT

pdctCod,

pdctNam,

txtDes

FROM

pdct

    INNER JOIN

pdctlines USING (pductlin);"

INNER JOIN with GROUP BY

The picture below contains two sample tables:

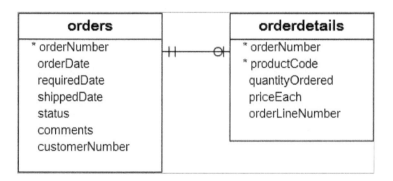

You could utilize this clause to obtain desired information from the two tables as shown in the two syntax below:

SELECT

  To1.orderNo,

  stats,

SUM(qtyOrdrd * pricEch) total
FROM
   order AS T01
      INNER JOIN
orderdetail AS T02 ON T01.orderNo = T02.orderNo
GROUP BY orderNo;

SELECT
orderNo,
   stats,
SUM(qtyOrdrd * pricEch) total
FROM
   order
      INNER JOIN
orderdetail USING (orderNo)
GROUP BY orderNo;"

A sample of the result set is shown in the picture below:

orderNumber	status	total
10100	Shipped	10223.83
10101	Shipped	10549.01
10102	Shipped	5494.78
10103	Shipped	50218.95
10104	Shipped	40206.20

MySQL INNER JOIN with Different Operators

We have only explored the join condition using the equal operator (=) to match the rows. But we can also use other operators with the join predicate including greater than (>), less than (<), and not-equal (<>) operators.

The syntax below utilizes a less than (<) operator to identify the sales price for the item with the code S11 1789, which are lower than the marked price.

```
SELECT
orderNo,
prdctNam,
mrp,
pricEch
FROM
    product x
        INNER JOIN
orderdetail y ON x.pdctcod = y.pdctcod
        AND x.mrp>y.pricEch
WHERE
x.pdctcode = 'S11_1789';
```

A sample of the result set is shown in the picture below:

orderNumber	productName	msrp	priceEach
10107	1969 Harley Davidson Ultimate Chopper	95.70	81.35
10121	1969 Harley Davidson Ultimate Chopper	95.70	86.13
10134	1969 Harley Davidson Ultimate Chopper	95.70	90.92
10145	1969 Harley Davidson Ultimate Chopper	95.70	76.56
10159	1969 Harley Davidson Ultimate Chopper	95.70	81.35
10168	1969 Harley Davidson Ultimate Chopper	95.70	94.74
10180	1969 Harley Davidson Ultimate Chopper	95.70	76.56
10201	1969 Harley Davidson Ultimate Chopper	95.70	82.30

LEFT JOIN

The MySQL LEFT JOIN enables querying of data from 2 or multiple tables on a database. The SELECT statement is not required to contain the LEFT JOIN clause for execution, which appears right next to the FROM clause. The principles of left table and right table are implemented when the 2 tables are linked, using the LEFT JOIN clause.

Unlike an INNER JOIN, these will return all rows in the left table, the rows meeting the condition and even the records not meeting the condition. The NULL value appears in the result set of the columns from the table on the right for records not meeting the condition.

Now, to further simplify this query we will assume that we are interested in linking only tables to1 and to2with the LEFT JOIN per the syntax below:

SELECT
to1.co1, to1.co2, to2.co1, to2.co2
FROM
to1
      LEFT JOIN
to2 ON to1.co1 = to2.co1;

In the syntax above, you are using the LEFT JOIN clause to connect the to1 to the to2, on the basis of a record from the table to1 on the left, aligning a record from the to2 on the right as defined by the join predicate (to1.co1= to2.co1), which are then included in the output.

If the record in the table on the left has no matching record that aligns with it in the table on the right, then the record in the table on the left will still be chosen and joined with a virtual record containing NULL values from the table on the right.

To put it simply, the LEFT JOIN clause enables selection of matching records from both the left and right tables, as well as all records from the left table (t01), even without aligning records from the right table (t02).

The Venn diagram shown in the picture below will help you understand how the working of the LEFT JOIN. The overlapping section of the two circles includes records that matched from the two tables, and the rest of the portion of the left circle includes rows in the t01 table with no corresponding record in the t02 table. Therefore, the output will include all records in the left table.

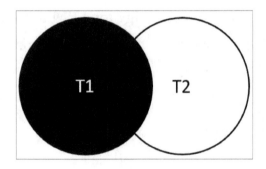

EXAMPLE

Consider the two tables, shown in the picture below, wherein every order value in the second table corresponds to a customer value in the first table but every customer value in the first table may not have a corresponding order value in the second table.

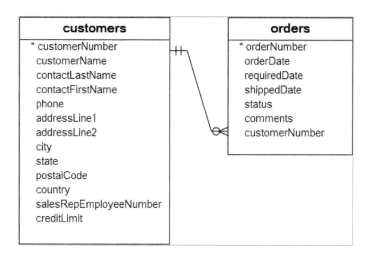

All the orders corresponding to a client can be queried using the LEFT JOIN clause using the syntax below:

SELECT
x.clientNo,
x.clientNam,
orderNo,
y.stats
FROM
clients x
LEFT JOIN order y ON x.clientNo = y.clientNo;"

The sample output is shown in the picture below, where the left table refers to the clients table, so all the rows with value in the clients table will be added to the output; although it contains rows with client data that have no order data such as

168 and 169. For such rows, the order data value is reflected as NULL implying that there is no order in the order table for those clients.

customerNumber	customerName	orderNumber	status
166	Handji Gifts& Co	10288	Shipped
166	Handji Gifts& Co	10409	Shipped
167	Herkku Gifts	10181	Shipped
167	Herkku Gifts	10188	Shipped
167	Herkku Gifts	10289	Shipped
168	American Souvenirs Inc	NULL	NULL
169	Porto Imports Co.	NULL	NULL
171	Daedalus Designs Imports	10180	Shipped
171	Daedalus Designs Imports	10224	Shipped
172	La Corne D'abondance, ...	10114	Shipped

Here's a tip!

Since both the tables share the column nameclientsNo, you could utilize the simpler query below (without the need of using the table aliases) and obtain the same output as shown in the picture above:

SELECT
x.clientNo,
x.clientNam,
orderNo,
 stats
FROM

clients x

LEFT JOINorder USING (clientNo);

MySQL LEFT JOIN with WHEREClause

Consider the syntax below with WHERE clause is used after the "LEFT JOIN" to retrieve desired information from the two tables.

SELECT
y.orderNo,
clientNo,
pdctCod
FROM
  Order y
    LEFT JOIN
orderDetail USING (orderNo)
WHERE
orderNo = 10125;

A sample of the "result set" is shown in the picture below for all the order number listed as 10123:

orderNumber	customerNumber	productCode
10123	103	S18_1589
10123	103	S18_2870
10123	103	S18_3685
10123	103	S24_1628

Note that if the join condition was changed from WHERE clause to the ON clause as shown in the syntax below, then the query will produce a different result set containing all orders but only the details associated with the order number 10125 will be displayed, similar to the picture below for 10123:

SELECT
y.orderNo,
clientNo,
pdctCod
FROM
  orders y
    LEFT JOIN
orderDetailz ON y.orderNo = y.orderNo
    AND y.orderNo = 10125;

orderNumber	customerNumber	productCode
10123	103	S18_1589
10123	103	S18_2870
10123	103	S18_3685
10123	103	S24_1628
10298	103	NULL
10345	103	NULL
10124	112	NULL
10278	112	NULL
10346	112	NULL
10120	114	NULL

RIGHT JOIN

The RIGHT JOIN or RIGHT OUTER JOIN is similar to the LEFT JOIN with the only difference being the treatment of the tables, which has been reversed from left to right. Each record from the table (to2) on the right appears in the output with a RIGHT JOIN. The NULL value will be displayed for columns in the table (to1) on the left for the records in the right table without any corresponding rows in the table (to1).

You could utilize the RIGHT JOIN clause to link tables to1 and to2 as illustrated in the syntax below:

SELECT
    *

FROM to1
    RIGHT JOIN to2 ON jn_predict;

In the syntax above, the right table is to2 and the left table is to1 and join_predicate indicated the matching criteria with which records from to1 will be aligned with records from to2.

With the execution of the query above, all the rows from the to2 will be displayed in the output and on the basis of the join condition, if no match are found for to2 with the rows of to1 then NULL value will be added to those columns from to1 table.

EXAMPLE

Let's consider the tables to1 and to2 as described in the syntax below:

CREATE TABLE to1 (
   id INT PRIMARY KEY,
ptrn VARCHAR(45) NOT NULL
);

CREATE TABLE to2 (
   id VARCHAR(45) PRIMARY KEY,
ptrnVARCHAR(45) NOT NULL
);

INSERT INTO to1(id, ptrn)

```
VALUES(01,'Pivot'),
    (02,'Bricks'),
    (03,'Grids');

INSERT INTO to2(id, pattern)
VALUES('A','Bricks'),
    ('B','Grids'),
    ('C','Diamonds');
```

The tables to1 and to2 can be joined with the pattern columns, as illustrated in the query below:

```
SELECT
to1.id, to2.id
FROM
to1
    RIGHT JOIN to2 USING (ptrn)
ORDER BY to2.id;
```

The result set is shown in the illustrated below:

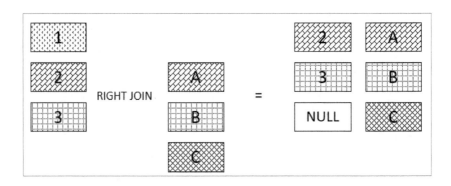

Or look at the syntax below to view the sales reps and their clients from the employee and client table:

SELECT
Cncat (h.fstNam,' ', h.lstNam) salesmn,
h.jobTitl,
clientNam
FROM
  employee h
    RIGHT JOIN
clients x ON h.employeeNo = x.salesRepEmployeeNo
    AND h.jobTitl = 'Sales Reps'
ORDER BY clientNam;

A sample of the result set is shown in the picture below:

salesman	jobTitle	customerName
▶ Gerard Hernandez	Sales Rep	Alpha Cognac
Foon Yue Tseng	Sales Rep	American Souvenirs Inc
Pamela Castillo	Sales Rep	Amica Models & Co.
NULL	NULL	ANG Resellers
Andy Fixter	Sales Rep	Anna's Decorations, Ltd
NULL	NULL	Anton Designs, Ltd.
NULL	NULL	Asian Shopping Network, Co
NULL	NULL	Asian Treasures, Inc.

CROSS JOIN

The CROSS JOIN clause is used to obtain a Cartesian product, which is defined as joining of each record of a table to each record of another. When this clause is utilized, the output contains all records from the two tables, which are a composite of the record from the 1st table and record from the 2nd table. This case exists only when a common link or column between the two tables that are joined cannot be found.

The biggest drawback is sheer volume of data, assume each table contains 1,000 rows, then the result set will contain 1,000x 1,000= 1,000,000 rows.

You could utilize the CROSS JOIN to join t01 and t02 as displayed in the syntax below:

```
SELECT
    *
FROM
To1
    CROSS JOIN
To2;
```

Unlike the RIGHT JOIN and LEFT JOIN, the CROSS JOIN can be operated without using a join predicate. Moreover, if the WHERE clause is added to the CROSS JOIN and the two tables to1 and to2 have a connection then it will operate as INNER JOIN, as displayed in the syntax below:

```
SELECT
    *
FROM
To1
    CROSS JOIN
To2
WHERE
To1.id = To2.id;
```

EXAMPLE

Let's use testdb database as described in the syntax below to better understand how the CROSS JOIN operates:

CREATE DATABASE IF NOT EXISTS testdb3;

USE testdb3;

CREATE TABLE pdct (
  id INT PRIMARY KEY AUTO_INCREMENT,
pdct_ nam VARCHAR(110),
pric DECIMAL(12, 3)
);

CREATE TABLE stre (
  id INT PRIMARY KEY AUTO_INCREMENT,
stre_ nam VARCHAR(110)
);

CREATE TABLE sale (
pdct_id INT,
stre_id INT,
  qty DECIMAL(12 , 3) NOT NULL,
sale_ dat DATE NOT NULL,
  PRIMARY KEY (pdct_id ,stre_id),

```
FOREIGN KEY (pdct_id)
    REFERENCES pdcts (id)
    ON DELETE CASCADE ON UPDATE CASCADE,
FOREIGN KEY (stre_id)
    REFERENCES stres (id)
    ON DELETE CASCADE ON UPDATE CASCADE
);
```

In the syntax above, we have 3 tables:

- The pdct table, which holds the fundamental data of the pdct including pdct id, pdct name, and sales pric.
- The stre table, which holds the data pertaining to the stores where the products are available for purchase.
- The sale table, which holds the data pertaining to the products sold in specific stores by date and quantity.

Let's assume there are 3 itemsMyPhone, Tablet and Comp available for selling 2 stores named North's and South's. We can populate the tables to hold this data using the syntax below:

```
INSERT INTO product(pdct_name, price)
VALUES('MyPhone', 899),
    ('Tablet', 499),
    ('Comp', 1599);

INSERT INTO stres(stre_name)
```

```
VALUES('North's'),
    ('South's');

INSERT INTO sale (stre_id,pdct_id, qty,sale_dat)
VALUES(10,10,200,'2018-02-03'),
    (10,20, 35, '2018-01-05'),
    (10, 30, 35,'2018-01-05'),
    (20 ,10 ,40,'2018-02-03'),
    (20, 20, 45,'2018-01-06');"
```

Now, to view the total sales for every product and store, the sales must be calculated first and then grouped by the store and product using the syntax below:

```
SELECT
stre_name,
pdct_name,
    SUM(qty * pric) AS rev
FROM
    sale
    INNER JOIN
pdct ON pdct.id = sale.pdct_id
    INNER JOIN
stres ON stres.id = sale.stre_id
GROUP BY stre_name ,pdct_name;
```

A sample of the result set is shown in the picture below:

store_name	product_name	revenue
North	iPad	8985.0000
North	iPhone	13980.0000
North	Macbook Pro	32475.0000
South	iPad	20965.0000
South	iPhone	20970.0000

Now, if you wanted to view the stores that had zero sale for a particular product, the syntax above will not provide you that information. This is where you can utilize the CROSS JOIN to first view a composite of all products and stores, as displayed in the query below:

SELECT
stre_name, pdct_name
FROM
stres AS p
    CROSS JOIN
pdct AS q;

A sample of the result set is shown in the picture in the next page:

store_name	product_name
North	iPhone
South	iPhone
North	iPad
South	iPad
North	Macbook Pro
South	Macbook Pro

And then, you can join the query result received earlier with this query that will result in the total sales by products and stores, using the syntax below:

SELECT

y.stre_name,

x.pdct_name,

   IFNULL(z.rev, a) AS rev

FROM

pdcts AS x

    CROSS JOIN

stres AS y

    LEFT JOIN

   (SELECT

stres.id AS stre_id,

pdcts.id AS pdct_id,

stre_name,

pdct_name,

     *ROUND(SUM (quantity * price), a) AS rev*

   FROM

sale

INNER JOIN pdcts ON pdcts.id = sales.pdct_id

INNER JOIN stres ON stres.id = sales.stre_id

GROUP BY stre_name ,pdct_name) AS c ON z.stre_id = y.id

   AND z.pdct_id= x.id

ORDER BY y.stre_name;

A sample of the result set is shown in the picture below:

store_name	product_name	revenue
North	Macbook Pro	32475
North	iPad	8985
North	iPhone	13980
South	iPhone	20970
South	Macbook Pro	0
South	iPad	20965

The IFNULL function was used in the syntax above to return 0 in case the revenue was reported as NULL.

SELF JOIN

As the name indicates, the SELF JOIN statements are utilized to link records of one table to records within the same table instead of another table. This requires you to use a table alias to aid the server in differentiating between the table on the left from the right within the same query. For instance, take the employees table in the "MySQL sample database" where structural data for the organization is stored along with the employee data, as shown in the picture below. The "reportsTo" column can be utilized to view the manager Id of any employee.

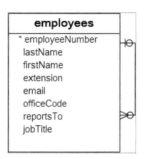

If you would like to view the complete org structure, you could self-join the employee table using employeeNo and reports to column, using the syntax below. The 2 roles in the employees table are Manager and Direct Reports.

SELECT
   CONCAT(n.lstname, ', ', n.fstname) AS 'Mgr',
   CONCAT(a.lstname, ', ', a.fstname) AS 'Drct rprt'
FROM
   Employee a
     INNER JOIN
   employee n ON n.employeeNo = a.reportsto
ORDER BY mgr;

A sample of the output is shown in the picture below:

Manager	Direct report
Bondur, Gerard	Jones, Barry
Bondur, Gerard	Bott, Larry
Bondur, Gerard	Castillo, Pamela
Bondur, Gerard	Hernandez, Gerard
Bondur, Gerard	Bondur, Loui
Bondur, Gerard	Gerard, Martin
Bow, Anthony	Tseng, Foon Yue
Bow, Anthony	Patterson, Steve
Bow, Anthony	Firrelli, Julie
Bow, Anthony	Thompson, Leslie
Bow, Anthony	Jennings, Leslie
Bow, Anthony	Vanauf, George

Only employees who are reporting to a manager can be seen in the result set above. But the lead manager is not visible as his name has been filtered out with the INNER JOIN clause. The lead manager is the manager who is not reporting to anyone or their manager no is holding a NULL value.

We can alter the INNER JOIN clause in the syntax above to the LEFT JOIN clause so it would include the lead manager in the output. If the name of the manager is holding a NULL value, you can utilize the "IFNULL" clause to include the lead manager in the output, as shown in the query below:

SELECT

```
IFNULL(CONCAT(n.lstname, ', ', n.fstname),
    'Lead Mgr') AS 'Mgr',
CONCAT(a.lstname, ', ', a.fstname) AS 'Drct rprt'
FROM
    Employee a
    LEFT JOIN
    employee n ON n.employeeNo = a.reportsto
ORDER BY mgr DESC;
```

A sample of the output is shown in the picture below:

Manager	Direct report
Top Manager	Murphy, Diane
Patterson, William	King, Tom
Patterson, William	Marsh, Peter
Patterson, William	Fixter, Andy
Patterson, Mary	Bondur, Gerard
Patterson, Mary	Nishi, Mami
Patterson, Mary	Patterson, William
Patterson, Mary	Bow, Anthony
Nishi, Mami	Kato, Yoshimi
Murphy, Diane	Firrelli, Jeff
Murphy, Diane	Patterson, Mary

You will be able to show a list of clients at a selected location by linking the clients table to itself with the use of the MySQL self join, as shown in the query below:

```
SELECT
    j1.cty, j1.clientName, j2.clientName
```

FROM

   clients j1

     INNER JOIN

clients j2 ON j1.cty = j2.cty

     AND j1.clientname> j2.clientName

ORDER BY j1.cty;"

A sample of the output is shown in the picture below:

city	customerName	customerName
Auckland	Kelly's Gift Shop	Down Under Souveniers, Inc
Auckland	GiftsForHim.com	Down Under Souveniers, Inc
Auckland	Kelly's Gift Shop	GiftsForHim.com
Boston	Gifts4AllAges.com	Diecast Collectables
Brickhaven	Online Mini Collectables	Auto-Moto Classics Inc.
Brickhaven	Collectables For Less Inc.	Auto-Moto Classics Inc.
Brickhaven	Online Mini Collectables	Collectables For Less Inc.
Cambridge	Marta's Replicas Co.	Cambridge Collectables Co.
Frankfurt	Messner Shopping Network	Blauer See Auto, Co.
Glendale	Gift Ideas Corp.	Boards & Toys Co.
Lisboa	Porto Imports Co.	Lisboa Souveniers, Inc
London	Stylish Desk Decors, Co.	Double Decker Gift Stores, Ltd

MySQL UNION

The UNION function in MySQL is used to merge multiple result sets to obtain one comprehensive output. The syntax for the UNION operator is given below:

SELECT col_list

UNION [DISTINCT | ALL]
SELECT col_list
UNION [DISTINCT | ALL]
SELECT col_list

.....

The fundamental rules to follow with the use of the UNION operator are:

- It is very critical that the number and the sequence of columns included in the SELECT statement is the same.
- The data types of the columns are required to be identical or convertible to the same.
- The redundant or duplicate rows will be removed without explicitly using the DISTINT function in the query.

EXAMPLE

Consider the sample tables to1 and to2 as described in the syntax below:

DROP TABLE IF EXISTS to1;
DROP TABLE IF EXISTS to2;

CREATE TABLE to1 (
  identity INT PRIMARY KEY

);

CREATE TABLE to2 (
identity INT PRIMARY KEY
);

INSERT INTO to1 VALUES (10),(20),(30);
INSERT INTO to2 VALUES (20),(30),(40);

The query below can be used to combine the result sets from to1 and to2 tables using the UNION operator:

SELECT identity
FROM to1
UNION
SELECT identity
FROM to2;

The combined output generated will contain varying values from both the result sets, as shown below:

```
+------+
| identity |
+------+
| 10 |
| 20 |
```

| 30 |
| 40 |
| 50 |
+------+

5 rows in set (0.3 sec)

One can notice that the rows containing values 2 and 3 are redundant, so the UNION function dropped the duplicate and retain the distinct values only. The picture below of the Venn diagram, represents the combination of the output from t01 and t02 tables:

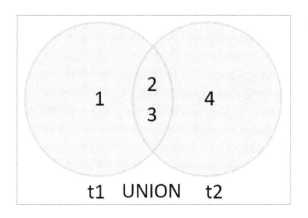

MySQL UNION ALL

The UNION ALL operator is utilized when you want to retain the duplicate rows (if any) in the output. The speed with which the query is executed is much higher for the UNION ALL operator than the UNION or UNION DISTINCT operator, as it does not need to deal with the redundancy of the data. The syntax for the UNION ALL operator is shown in the query below:

SELECT identity
FROM to1
UNION ALL
SELECT identity
FROM to2;

The result set is given below, which contains duplicate rows:

```
+------+
| identity |
+------+
| 10 |
| 20 |
| 50 |
| 30 |
| 20 |
| 30 |
| 40 |
+----+
```
7 rows in set (0.02 sec)

MySQL JOIN vs UNION

The JOIN clause is utilized to merge the result sets horizontally or on the basis of the rows or records. On the other hand, the UNION clause is utilized to merge the result sets vertically or on the basis of the columns of the tables. The picture below will help you understand the distinction between UNION and JOIN operators:

MySQL UNION and ORDER BY

This clause can be utilized to sort the results of a UNION operator as shown the query below:

SELECT
conct(fstName,' ',lstName) fulname
FROM
  employee

UNION SELECT

conct(cntctFstName,' ',cntctLstName)

FROM

clients

ORDER BY fulname;

A sample of the output is shown in the picture below:

If you would like to sort the result on the basis of a column position, you could utilize the ORDER BY by executing the syntax below:

SELECT

conct (fstName,' ',lstName) fulname

FROM

  employee

UNION SELECT

conct (cntctFstName,' ',cntctLstName)

FROM

clients

ORDER BY 2;

Chapter 4:SQL Views and Transactions

A Database View in SQL is defined as a "virtual or logical table" described as the SELECT statements containing join function. As a Database View is like a table in the database consisting of rows and columns, you will be able to easily run queries on it. Many DBMSs, including MySQL, enable users to modify information in the existing tables using Database View by meeting certain prerequisites, as shown in the picture below.

A SQL database View can be deemed dynamic since there is no connection between the SQL View to the physical system. The database system will store SQL Views in the form on SELECT statements using JOIN clause. When the information in the table is modified, the SQL View will also reflect that modification.

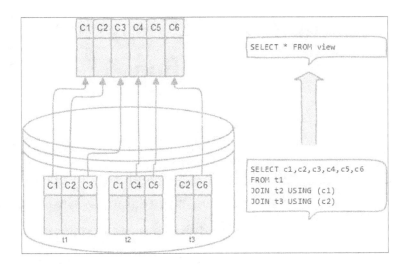

Pros of Using SQL View

- A SQL View enables simplification of complicated queries: a SQL View is characterized by a SQL statement which is associated with multiple tables. To conceal the complexity of the underlying tables from the end-users and external apps, SQL View is extremely helpful. You only need to use straightforward SQL statements instead of complicated ones with multiple JOIN clauses using the SQL View.

- A SQL View enables restricted access to information depending on the user requirements. Perhaps you would not like all users to be able to query a subset of confidential information. In such cases SQL View can be used to selectively expose non-sensitive information to a targeted set of users.

- The SQL View offers an additional layer of safety. Data security is a key component of every DBMS. It ensures additional security for the DBMS. It enables generation of a read only view to display read only information for targeted users. In read only view, users are able to only retrieve data and are not allowed to update any information.

- The SQL View is used to enable computed columns. The table in the database is not capable of containing computed columns but a SQL View can easily contain computed column. Assume in the OrderDetails table there is the quantity Order column for the amount of products ordered and priceEach column for the price of each item. But the OrderDetails table cannot contain a calculated column storing total sales for every product from the order. If it could, the database schema may have never been a good design. In such a situation, to display the calculated outcome, you could generate a computed column called total, which would be a product of quantityOrder and priceEach columns. When querying information from the SQL View, the calculated column information will be calculated on the fly.

- A SQL View allows for backward compatibility. Assume that we have a central database that is being used by multiple applications. Out of the blue you have been tasked to redesign the database accommodating the new business needs. As you delete some tables and create new ones, you would not want other applications to be affected by these modifications. You could generate SQL Views in such situations, using the identical schematic of the legacy tables that you are planning to delete.

Cons of Using SQL View

In addition to the pros listed above, the use of SQL View may have certain disadvantages such as:

- Performance: Executing queries against SQL View could be slow, particularly if it is generated from another SQL View.
- Table dependencies: Since a SQL View is created from the underlying tables of the database. Anytime the tables structure connected with SQL View is modified, you also need to modify the SQL View.

Views in MySQLServer

As of the release of MySQL version 5+, it has been supporting database views. In MySQL, nearly all characteristics of a View conform to the standard SQL: 2003.

MySQL can run queries against the views in couple of ways:

1. MySQL can produce a temp table based on the "view definition statement" and then execute all following queries on this temp table.
2. MySQL can combine the new queries with the query that specifies the SQL View into a single comprehensive query and then this merged query can be executed.

MySQL offers versioning capability for all SQL Views. Whenever a SQL View is modified or substituted, its clone is backed up in the arc (archive) directory residing in a particular folder, which is named view name.frm-0001. If the view is modified in future, then MySQL would generate a new backup file called view name.frm-0002.

You can also generate a view based on other views through MySQL, by creating references for other views in the SELECT statement defining the target SQL View.

CREATE VIEW in MySQL

The CREATE VIEW query can be utilized to generate new SQL Views in MySQL, as shown in the syntax below:

CREATE
 [ALGRTHM = {MRG | TEMPTAB | UNDEFND}]
VIEW view_nam [(col_lst)]
AS
select statmnt;

"View Processing Algorithms"

The attribute of the algorithm enables you to regulate which mechanism is utilized by MySQL to create the SQL View. Three algorithms are provided by MySQL, namely: MERGE, TEMPTABLE and UNDEFINED.

- To use the MERGE algorithm, server will start by combining the incoming queries with the SELECT statement, that will define the view into a merged query. Subsequently, the merged query is executed by MySQL to retrieve the output. This algorithm cannot be used if the SELECT statements consist of aggregate functions like "MIN, MAX, SUM, COUNT, AVG or DISTINCT, GROUP BY, HAVING, LIMIT, UNION, UNION ALL, subquery." If these statements do not refer to a table, then this algorithm cannot be utilized. In the cases, where the MERGE algorithm is not permitted, server will instead use the UNDEFINED algorithm. Please remember that the view resolution is defined as a combo of input queries and the view definition queries into one.

- Using the TEMPTABLE algorithm, server will start with production of a temporary table that describes the SQL View on the basis of the SELECT statement. Subsequently any incoming query will be executed against this temp table. This algorithm has lower efficiency than the "MERGE" algorithm because MySQL requires generation of a temp table to save the output and will transfer the data from the standard table to the temp. Moreover, a SQL View using the TEMPTABLE algorithm cannot be updated.

- If you generate a view without explicitly stating an algorithm that needs to be used, then the UNDEFINED algorithm will be used by default. The UNDEFINED algorithm allows MySQL to choose from the MERGE or TEMPTABLE algorithm to be used. Since the MERGE algorithm is much more effective, MySQL prefers MERGE algorithm over TEMPTABLE algorithm.

View Name

Views and tables are stored in the same space within the database, so it is not possible to give the same name to a view and a table. Furthermore, the name of a view has to be in accordance with the naming conventions of the table.

SELECT statements

It is easy to retrieve desired data from tables or views contained within a database by utilizing these statements.

These statements are required to meet various guidelines, such as:

- It may comprise of sub-queries in the "WHERE" clause but cannot have any in the "FROM" clause.
- No variables, including session variables, local variables, user variables, and, can be referred to in these statements.
- These statements can also not have a reference to the parameters of prepared statements and is not required to refer to any other table.

EXAMPLE

To generate a view of the orderDetail table that contains the total sales per order, you can use the query below:

```
CREATE VIEW SalePrOrdr AS
   SELECT
orderNo, SUM(qtyOrdrd * pricEch) total
   FROM
orderDetail
   GROUP by orderNo
   ORDER BY totl DESC;
```

By using the "SHOW TABLE" command you can check all the tables in the classic model database, it is easily visible that the SalesPrOrdr view is on the displayed list (shown in the picture below):

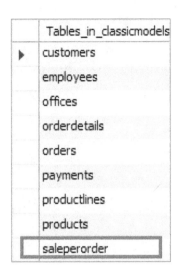

Tables_in_classicmodels
customers
employees
offices
orderdetails
orders
payments
productlines
products
saleperorder

This proves that the view names and table names are stored in the same space within the database. So, now if you would like to know which object in the picture above is view or table, use the "SHOW FULL TABLE" query and the output will be displayed as shown in the picture below:

Tables_in_classicmodels	Table_type
customers	BASE TABLE
employees	BASE TABLE
offices	BASE TABLE
orderdetails	BASE TABLE
orders	BASE TABLE
payments	BASE TABLE
productlines	BASE TABLE
products	BASE TABLE
saleperorder	VIEW

You can check the table_type column in the picture above to confirm objects that may be views or tables.

Now, you can simply utilize these statements below to view total sales for each sales order:

SELECT

     *

FROM

salePrOrdr;

The output is displayed in the picture below:

orderNumber	total
10165	67392.84
10287	61402
10310	61234.66
10212	59830.54
10207	59265.14
10127	58841.35
10204	58793.53
10126	57131.92

Creating a SQL View from Another SQL View

The MySQL server permits creation of a new view on the basis of another view. For instance, you could produce a view named BigSalesOrdr based on the SalesPrOrdr view, that we created earlier to show every sales order for which the total adds up to more than 61,000 using the syntax below:

CREATE VIEW BigSalesOrdr AS
   SELECT
orderNo, ROUND (totl, 3) as total
   FROM
saleprordr
   WHERE
totl> 61000;

You could easily retrieve desired data from the BigSalesOrdr view as shown below:

SELECT
orderNo, totl
FROM
BigSalesOrdr;

orderNumber	total
▶ 10165	67392.85
10287	61402.00
10310	61234.67

Create SQL View with JOIN Clause

The MySQL database allows you to create SQL View using JOIN clause. For instance, the query below with the INNER JOIN clause can be used to create a view containing order no, client name, and totl sale per ordr:

CREATE VIEW clientOrdrs AS
  SELECT
x.orderNo,
clientName,
  *SUM(qtyOrdrd * pricEch) total*
  FROM
orderDetail d
    INNER JOIN
  order r ON r.orderNo = x.orderNo
    INNER JOIN
  clients y ON y.clientNo = y.clientNo
  GROUP BY x.orderNo

ORDER BY totl DESC;

By executing the syntax below, the desired data can be retrieved from the client order view:

SELECT *FROM
clientOrder;

The result set is displayed in the picture below:

orderNumber	customerName	total
10165	Dragon Souveniers, Ltd.	67392.84
10287	Vida Sport, Ltd	61402
10310	Toms Spezialitäten, Ltd	61234.66
10212	Euro+ Shopping Channel	59830.54
10207	Diecast Collectables	59265.14
10127	Muscle Machine Inc	58841.35
10204	Muscle Machine Inc	58793.53
10126	Corrida Auto Replicas, Ltd	57131.92

Create SQL View with a Subquery

The query below can be used to generate a SQL View with a subquery, containing products with purchase prices greater than the average product prices.

CREATE VIEW abvAvgPdcts AS
  SELECT
pdctCode, pdctName, buyPric

162

FROM

pdcts

   WHERE

buyPric>

 (SELECT

AVG(buyPric)

     FROM

pdcts)

   ORDER BY buyPric DESC;

The query to extract data from the aboveAvgPdcts view is even more straightforward, as shown in the picture below:

SELECT

   *

FROM

abvAvgPdcts;

The result set is displayed in the picture below:

productCode	productName	buyPrice
S10_4962	1962 LanciaA Delta 16V	103.42
S18_2238	1998 Chrysler Plymouth Prowler	101.51
S10_1949	1952 Alpine Renault 1300	98.58
S24_3856	1956 Porsche 356A Coupe	98.3
S12_1108	2001 Ferrari Enzo	95.59
S12_1099	1968 Ford Mustang	95.34
S18_1984	1995 Honda Civic	93.89
S18_4027	1970 Triumph Spitfire	91.92

Updatable SQL Views

The MySQL server offers the capability to not only query the view but also to update them. The INSERT or UPDATE statements can be used add and edit the records of the underlying table through the updatable MySQL View. Moreover, the DELETE statement can be used to drop records from the underlying table through the updatable MySQL View.

Furthermore, the SELECT statement used to generate and define an updatable view can not include any of the functions listed below:

- "Aggregate functions" such as "MIN, MAX, SUM, AVG, and COUNT."
- "DISTINCT, GROUP BY, HAVING, UNION or UNION ALL, LEFT JOIN or OUTER JOIN."
- Subquery in the WHERE clauses or SELECT statements referring to the table indicated in the FROM clauses.
- References to non-updatable views in the FROM clause.
- References only to literal values.

Remember, the TEMPTABLE algorithm cannot be used to generate an updatable MySQL View.

EXAMPLE

You can use the syntax below to generate a view called ofcInfo on the basis of the ofc table. This updatable view will refer to 3 columns of the ofcs table: ofcCode, phne, and cty.

CREATE VIEW ofcInfo
 AS
  SELECT ofcCode, phne, cty
  FROM ofcs;

Now, if you would like to query the data from the ofcInfo view, you can easily do that by using the syntax below:

SELECT
  *

FROM
ofcInfo;

The result set is displayed in the picture below:

officeCode	phone	city
1	+1 650 219 4782	San Francisco
2	+1 215 837 0825	Boston
3	+1 212 555 3000	NYC
4	+33 14 723 4404	Paris
5	+81 33 224 5000	Tokyo
6	+61 2 9264 2451	Sydney
7	+44 20 7877 2041	London

You could also update the office contact number with ofcCode 4 using the UPDATE statement as given below, on the ofcInfo view:

UPDATE ofcInfo
SET
phne = '+1 24 763 5345'
WHERE
ofcCode = 3;

Lastly, you can confirm this modification, using the syntax below to retrieve desired data from the ofcInfo view:

SELECT
    *

FROM
ofcInfo
WHERE

ofcCode = 2;

A sample of the output for code = 4, is displayed in the picture below:

	officeCode	phone	city
▶	4	+33 14 723 5555	Paris

Check if an Existing View is Updatable

By running a query against the is_updtble column from the view in the info_schema database, you should verify whether a view in the database is updatable or not.

You can use the query below to display all the views from the classicmodeldb and check which for views that can be updated:

SELECT
tab_name,
is_updtble
FROM
info_schema.view
WHERE

tab_schema = 'classicmodel';

The result set is displayed in the picture below:

table_name	is_updatable
aboveavgproducts	YES
customerorders	NO
officeinfo	YES
saleperorder	NO

Dropping Rows Using SQL View

To understand this concept, execute the syntax below to first create a table called itms, use the INSERT statements to add records into this table and then use the CREATE clause to generate a view containing items with prices higher than 701.

--- creating new tbl called itms
CREATE TABLE itms (
*   identity INT AUTO_INCREMENT PRIMARY KEY,*
nam VARCHAR (110) NOT NULL,
pric DECIMAL (10 , 1) NOT NULL
)

-- addingrecords into itmstbl
INSERT INTO itms (nam,pric)

VALUES ('Comp', 600.54), ('Laptop', 799.99),('Tablet', 699.50)
;

--- creating views based on itmstbl
CREATE VIEW LxryItms AS
   SELECT
      *
   FROM
itms
   WHERE
pric> 899;
--- retrieve records from the LxryItms view
SELECT
   *
FROM
LxryItms;

The result set is displayed in the picture below:

	id	name	price
▶	1	Laptop	700.56
	3	iPad	700.50

Now, using the DELETE clause record with identity value 3 can be dropped.

DELETE FROM LxryItms

WHERE

id = 3;

After you run the query above, you will receive a message stating 1 row(s) affected.

Now, to verify the data with the view use the query below:

SELECT

    *

FROM

LxryItms;

The result set is displayed in the picture below:

	id	name	price
▶	1	Laptop	700.56

Finally, use the syntax below to retrieve desired records from the underlying table to confirm that the "DELETE" statement in fact removed the record:

SELECT

    *

FROM

itms;

The result set is displayed in the picture below, which confirms that the record with identity value 3 has been deleted from the items table:

id	name	price
1	Laptop	700.56
2	Desktop	699.99

Modification of SQL View

In MySQL, you can use ALTER VIEW and CREATE OR REPLACE VIEW statements to make changes to views that have already been created.

Using ALTER VIEWStatement

The syntax for ALTER VIEW works a lot like the CREATE VIEW statement that you learned earlier, the only difference being that the ALTER keyword is used instead of the CREATE keyword, as shown below:

```
ALTER
[ALGRTHM = {MERG | TEMPTBL | UNDEFND}]
 VIEW [db_nam]. [vw_nam]
  AS
[SELECT  statemnt]
```

The query below will change the organization view by
incorporating the email column in the table:

```
ALTER VIEW org
 AS
 SELECT CONCAT (x.lastname,x.firstname) AS Emplye,
x.emailAS  emplyeEmail,
CONCAT(y.lstname, y.fstname) AS Mgr
 FROM emplyes AS x
 INNER JOIN emplyes AS y
  ON y.emplyeNo = x.ReprtsTo
 ORDER BY Mgr;
```

You may run the code below against the org view to verify the
modification:

```
SELECT
   *
FROM
  Org;
```

The result set is displayed in the picture below:

	Employee	employeeEmail	Manager
▶	JonesBarry	bjones@classicmodelcars.com	BondurGerard
	HernandezGerard	ghernande@classicmodelcars.com	BondurGerard
	BottLarry	lbott@classicmodelcars.com	BondurGerard
	GerardMartin	mgerard@classicmodelcars.com	BondurGerard
	BondurLoui	lbondur@classicmodelcars.com	BondurGerard
	CastilloPamela	pcastillo@classicmodelcars.com	BondurGerard
	VanaufGeorge	gvanauf@classicmodelcars.com	BowAnthony

Using CREATE OR REPLACE VIEW Statement

These statements can be used to replace or generate a SQL View that already exists in the database. For all existing views, MySQL will easily modify the view but if the view is non-existent, it will create a new view based on the query.

The syntax below can be used to generate the contacts view on the basis of the employees table:

CREATE OR REPLACE VIEW cntcts AS
*   SELECT*
fstName, lstName, extnsn, eml
*   FROM*

173

emplyes;

The result set is displayed in the picture below:

	firstName	lastName	extension	email
▶	Diane	Murphy	x5800	dmurphy@classicmodelcars.com
	Mary	Patterson	x4611	mpatterso@classicmodelcars.com
	Jeff	Firrelli	x9273	jfirrelli@classicmodelcars.com
	William	Patterson	x4871	wpatterson@classicmodelcars.com
	Gerard	Bondur	x5408	gbondur@classicmodelcars.com
	Anthony	Bow	x5428	abow@classicmodelcars.com
	Leslie	Jennings	x3291	ljennings@classicmodelcars.com

Now, assume that you would like to insert the jobtitl column to the cntcts view. You can accomplish this with the syntax below:

CREATE OR REPLACE VIEW cntcts AS
   SELECT
fstName, lstName, extnsn, eml, jobtitl
   FROM
emplyes;

The result set is displayed in the picture below:

firstName	lastName	extension	email	jobtitle
Diane	Murphy	x5800	dmurphy@classicmodelcars.com	President
Mary	Patterson	x4611	mpatterso@classicmodelcars.com	VP Sales
Jeff	Firrelli	x9273	jfirrelli@classicmodelcars.com	VP Marketing
William	Patterson	x4871	wpatterson@classicmodelcars.com	Sales Manager (APAC)
Gerard	Bondur	x5408	gbondur@classicmodelcars.com	Sale Manager (EMEA)
Anthony	Bow	x5428	abow@classicmodelcars.com	Sales Manager (NA)
Leslie	Jennings	x3291	ljennings@classicmodelcars.com	Sales Rep

Dropping a SQL View

The DROP VIEW statement can be utilized to delete an existing
view from the database, using the syntax below:

DROP VIEW [IF EXISTS] [db_name]. [vw_name]

The "IF EXISTS" clause is not mandatory in the statement above
and is used to determine if the view already exists in the
database. It prevents you from mistakenly removing a view that
does not exists in the database.

You may, for instance, use the DROP VIEW statement as shown
in the syntax below to delete the organization view:

DROP VIEW IF EXISTS org;

SQL TRANSACTIONS

Any actions that are executed on a database are called as transactions. These are actions that are executed logically, either manually by a user or automatically using by the database program.

Or simply put, they are the spread of one or more database modifications. For instance, every time you create a row, update a row, or delete a row a transaction is being executed on that table. To maintain data integrity and address database errors, it is essential to regulate these transactions.

Basically, to execute a transaction, you must group several SQL queries and run them at the same time.

Properties of Transactions

The fundamental properties of a transaction can be defined using the acronym **ACID** for the properties listed below:

- **Atomicity** – guarantees successful completion of all operations grouped in the work unit. Or else, at the point of failure, the transaction will be aborted, and all prior operations will be rolled back to their original state.

- **Consistency** – makes sure that when a transaction is properly committed, the database states are also correctly updated.

- **Isolation** – allows independent and transparent execution of the transactions.

- **Durability** – makes sure that in case of a system malfunction, the outcome or impact of a committed transaction continues to exist.

To explain this concept in greater detail, consider the steps below for addition of new sales orders:

- Start by querying the most recent sales ordr no from the ordrs table and utilize the subsequent ordr no as the new ordr no.
- Then use the INSERT clause to add a new sales ordr into the ordrs table.
- Next, retrieve the sales ordr no that was inserted in the previous step.
- Now, INSERT the new ordritms into the order detail table containing the order no.
- At last, to verify the modifications, select data from the ordrs table as well as the order detail table.

Imagine how would the sales order data be modified, if even a single step listed here were to fail, for whatever reason. For instance, if the step for inserting items of an order to the order detail table failed, it will result in a blank sales ordr.

This is where the "transaction processing" is used as a safety measure. You can perform MySQL transactions to run a set of operations making sure that the database will not be able to contain any partial operations. When working with multiple operations concurrently, if even one of the operations fails, a rollback can be triggered. If there is no failure, all the statements will be committed to the db.

MySQL Transaction Statements

MySQL offers statements listed below for controlling the transactions:

- For initiating a transaction, utilize the START/ BEGIN/ BEGIN WORK TRANSACTION statements.
- For committing the latest transactions and making the modifications permanent, utilize the COMMIT declaration.

- By using the ROLLBACK declaration, you can simply undo the current transaction and void its modifications.
- By using the SET autocommit statement, you can deactivate or activate the auto commit mode for the current transaction.

By default, MySQL is designed to commit the modifications to the database permanently. By using the statement below, you can force MySQL not to commit the modifications by default:

SET auto commit = 1;
Or
SET autocommit = OFF;

To reactivate the default mode for auto-commit, you can use the syntax below:

SET autocommit = ON;

EXAMPLE

Let's utilize the orders and orderDetails tables, shown in the picture below, from the MySQL sample database to understand this concept further.

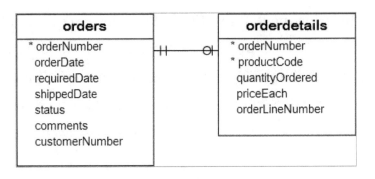

COMMIT Transaction

You must first split the SQL statement into logical parts to effectively use a transaction and assess when the transaction needs to be committed or rolled back.

The steps below show how to generate a new sales order:

1. Utilize the START TRANSACTION statement to begin a transaction.
2. Select the most recent sales ordr no from the ordrs table and utilize the subsequent ordr no as the new ordr no.
3. Add a new record in the ordrs table.
4. Add sales order items into the order detail table.
5. Lastly, commit the transaction.

You could potentially use data from ordrs and order detail table to verify the new ordr, as shown in the syntax below:

initiate new transactions
START TRANSACTION;

Retrieve the most recent ordr no
SELECT
  @ordrNo:=MAX (ordrNo)+2
FROM
ordrs;

add a new record for customer 140
INSERT INTO ordrs(ordrNo,
ordrDat,
reqrdDat,
shipdDat,
sttus,
clientNo)
VALUES(@ordrNo,
    '2015-05-31',
    '2015-06-10',
    '2015-06-11',
    'In Process',
    140);

Add ordr line itms

INSERT INTO ordrdetail(ordrNo,

pdctCode,

qtyOrdrd,

pricEch,

ordrLineNo)

VALUES(@ordrNo, 'S19_1748', 20, '135', 2),

   (@ordrNo, 'S19_2349', 40, '45', 2);

commitingupdates

COMMIT;

The result set is displayed in the picture below:

	@orderNumber:=IFNULL(MAX(orderNUmber),0)+1
▶	10426

Using the query below, you can retrieve the new sales order that you just created:

SELECT

x.ordrNumber,

ordrDate,

rqrdDate,

shipdDate,

sttus,

cmnts,

clientNo,

ordrLineNo,

pdctCode,

qtyOrdrd,

pricEch

FROM

ordrs x

    INNER JOIN

ordrdetail y USING (ordrNumber)

WHERE

x.ordrno = 10426;

The result set is displayed in the picture below:

orderNumber	orderDate	requiredDate	shippedDate	status	comments	customerNumber	orderLineNumber	productCode	quantityOrdered	priceEach
10426	2005-05-31	2005-06-10	2005-06-11	In Process	NULL	145	1	S18_1749	30	136.00
10426	2005-05-31	2005-06-10	2005-06-11	In Process	NULL	145	2	S18_2248	50	55.09

ROLLBACK Transaction

The first step here is deletion of the data in the ordrs table, using the statement below:

START TRANSACTION;

Query OK, 0 record affctd (0.01 sec)

DELETE FROM ordrs;

Query OK, 310 record affcted (0.02 sec)

It's obvious from from the output of the queries above that all records from the "orders" table have been removed.

Now, you need to login to the MySQL in a distinct session and run the statement below against the ordrstable.

SELECT COUNT (*) FROM ordrs;

+--------+

| COUNT (*)

+--------+

| 311 |

+--------+

2 rows in set (0.02 secs)

The data from the ordrs table can still be viewed from the second session.

The updates made in the first session are not permanent, so you need to either commit them or roll them back. Let's assume you would like to undo the changes from the first session, utilize the query below:

ROLLBACK;

Query OK, 2 rows affected (0.07 secs)"

The data in the ordrs table from the first session can be verified, using the syntax below:

SELECT COUNT (*) FROM ordrs;

+--------+

| COUNT(*) |

+--------+

| 311 |

+--------+

2 rows in set (0.10 secs)

It can be seen in the result set above that the modifications have been rolled back.

SAVEPOINT Transaction

The SAVEPOINT is defined as transaction points when the transaction can be rolled back to a predefined point without rolling it back completely, as shown in the syntax below:

SAVEPOINT SVEPNT_NAME;

The query above is only used to create a SAVEPOINT within all the transaction statements and then the ROLLBACK query can be utilized to retract desired transactions, as shown in the query below:

ROLLBACK TO SVPNT_NAME;

For example, assume you have a client's table as shown in the picture below and want to delete 3 rows and create a SAVEPOINT prior to every deletion and then subsequent ROLLBACK the change to the preceding state as needed.

```
+----+----------+-----+-----------+----------+
| ID | NAME     | AGE | ADDRESS   | SALARY   |
+----+----------+-----+-----------+----------+
|  1 | Ramesh   |  32 | Ahmedabad |  2000.00 |
|  2 | Khilan   |  25 | Delhi     |  1500.00 |
|  3 | kaushik  |  23 | Kota      |  2000.00 |
|  4 | Chaitali |  25 | Mumbai    |  6500.00 |
|  5 | Hardik   |  27 | Bhopal    |  8500.00 |
|  6 | Komal    |  22 | MP        |  4500.00 |
|  7 | Muffy    |  24 | Indore    | 10000.00 |
+----+----------+-----+-----------+----------+
```

You can accomplish this by running the queries below:

SQL> SAVEPOINT SP001;
Save point generated

SQL> DELETE FROM CLIENTS WHERE ID= 001;
2 rows deleted.

SQL> SAVEPOINT SP002;
Save point generated

SQL> DELETE FROM CLIENTS WHERE ID= 002;
0 row deleted.

SQL> SAVEPOINT SP3;
Save point generated

SQL> DELETE FROM CLIENTS WHERE ID= 003;
2 rows deleted.

With the query above, you have successfully deleted 3 records and are now ready to use the query below to ROLLBACK the change to the SAVEPOINT named SP002, which was generated post first deletion so the last 2 deletions will be rolled back:

SQL> ROLLBACK TO SP002;
Rolling back has been completed.

The result set is displayed in the picture below:

```
ID | NAME      | AGE | ADDRESS    | SALARY
---+-----------+-----+------------+----------
 2 | Khilan    |  25 | Delhi      |  1500.00
 3 | kaushik   |  23 | Kota       |  2000.00
 4 | Chaitali  |  25 | Mumbai     |  6500.00
 5 | Hardik    |  27 | Bhopal     |  8500.00
 6 | Komal     |  22 | MP         |  4500.00
 7 | Muffy     |  24 | Indore     | 10000.00
```

RELEASE SAVEPOINT Transaction

It can be utilized to delete a save point that might have been generated earlier, as shown in the syntax below:

RELEASE SAVEPOINT SVPNT_NAME;

Remember, once you run the query above there is no function to undo the transactions that might have been executed after the last save point.

SET TRANSACTION

It can be utilized to start a transaction by specifying features of the subsequent transactions. For instance, using the syntax below, a transaction can be made read and write only:

SET TRANSACTION [READ WRITE | READ ONLY];

SQL BACKUP DATABASE Statement

These statements can be utilized to generate a full back up of a database that already exists on the SQL server, as displayed in the syntax below:

BACKUP DATABASE dbname
TO DISK = 'flpth';

SQL BACKUP WITH DIFFERENTIAL Statement

A "differential backup" is used to selectively back up the sections of the database which were altered after the last full backup of the database, as displayed in the syntax below:

BACKUP DATABASE dbname
TO DISK = 'flpth'
WITH DIFFERENTIAL;

EXAMPLE

Consider that you have a database called testDB2 and you would like to create a full back up of it. To accomplish this, you can use the query below:

BACKUP DATABASE testDB2

TO DISK = 'c:\backup\testDB2.bak';

Now, if you made modifications to the database after running the query above. You can use the query below to create a backup of those modifications:

BACKUP DATABASE testDB2

TO DISK = 'c:\backup\testDB2.bak'

WITH DIFFERENTIAL;

Chapter 5: Database Security and Administration

MySQL has an integrated advanced access control and privilege system that enables generation of extensive access guidelines for user activities and efficiently prevent unauthorized users from getting access to the database system.

There are 2 phases in MySQL access control system for when a user is connected to the server:

- **Connection verification**: Every user is required to have valid username and password, that is connected to the server. Moreover, the host used by the user to connect must be the same as the one used in the MySQL grant table.
- **Request verification**: After a link has been effectively created for every query executed by the user, MySQL will verify if the user has required privileges to run that` specific query. MySQL is capable of checking user privileges at database, table, and field level.

The MySQL installer will automatically generate a database called mysql. The mysql database is comprised of 5 main grant tables. Using GRANT and REVOKE statements like, these tables can be indirectly manipulated.

- **User**: This includes columns for user accounts and global privileges. MySQL either accepts or rejects a connection from the host using these user tables. A privilege given under the user table is applicable to all the databases on the server.

- **Database**: This comprises of db level privilege. MySQL utilizes the "db_table" to assess the database that can be used by a user to access and to host the connection. These privileges are applicable to the particular database and all the object available in that database, such as stored procedures, views, triggers, tables, and many more.

- **"Table_priv" and "columns_priv"**: This includes privileges at the level of column and table. A privilege given in the "table priv" table is applicable only to that columns of that particular table, on the other hand privileges given in the "columns priv" table is applicable only to that particular column.

- **"Procs_priv"**: This includes privileges for saved functions and processes.

MySQL uses the tables listed above to regulate MySQL database server privileges. It is extremely essential to understand these tables before implementing your own dynamic access control system.

Creating User Accounts

In MySQL you can indicate that the user has been privileged to connect to the database server as well as the host to be used by the user to build that connection. As a result, for every user account a username and a host name in MySQL is generated and divided by the @ character.

For instance, if an admin user is connected from a localhost to the server, the user account will be named as "admin@localhost." However, the "admin_user" is allowed to connect only to the server using a "localhost" or a remote host like mysqlearn.org, which ensures that the server has higher security.

Moreover, by merging the username and host, various accounts with the same name can be configured and still possess the ability to connect from distinct hosts while being given distinct privileges, as needed.

In the mysql database all the user accounts are stored in the "user grant" table.

Using MySQL CREATE USER Statement

The "CREATE USER" is utilized with the MySQL server to setup new user accounts, as shown in the syntax below:

CREATE USER usr_acnt IDENTIFY BY paswrd;

In the syntax above, the CREATE USER clause is accompanied by the name of the user account in username @ hostname format.

In the "IDENTIFIED BY" clause, the user password would be indicated. It is important that the password is specified in plain text. Prior to the user account being saved in the user table, MySQL is required for encryption of the user passwords.

For instance, these statements can be utilized as given below, for creating a new "user dbadmin," that is connected to the server from local host using user password as Safe.

CREATE USER dbadmn@lclhst
IDENTIFY BY 'Safe';

If you would like to check the permissions given to any user account, you can run the syntax below:

SHOW GRANTS FOR dbadmn@localhst and dbadmn2@localhst2;

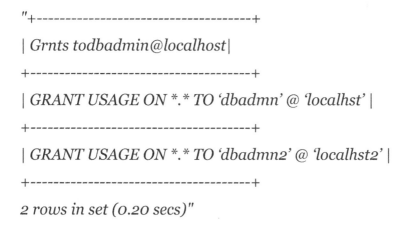

The *. * in the output above indicates that the dbadmn and dbadmn2 users are allowed to log into the server only and do not have any other access privileges.

Bear in mind that the portion prior to the dot (.) is representing the db and the portion following the dot is representing the table, for example, db.tab.

The percentage (%) wildcard can be used as shown in the syntax below for allowing a user to create a connection from any host:

CREATE USER supradmn@'%'
IDENTIFY BY 'safe';

The percentage (%) wildcard will lead to identical result as when included in the "LIKE" operator, for example, to enable msqladmn user account to link to the server from any "subdomain" of the mysqlearn.org host, this can be used as shown in the syntax below:

```
CREATE USER 'msqladmn@' % 'mysqlearn.org'
IDENTIFT by 'safe';"
```

It should also be noted here, that another wildcard underscore (_) can be used in the CREATE USER statement.

If the host name portion can be omitted from the user accounts, server will recognize them and enable the users to get connected from other hosts. For instance, the syntax below will generate a new remote user account that allows creation of a connection to from random hosts:

CREATE USER remoteuser;

To view the privileges given to the remoteuser and remoteuser2 account, you can use the syntax below:

SHOW GRANTS FOR remoteuser, remoteuser2;

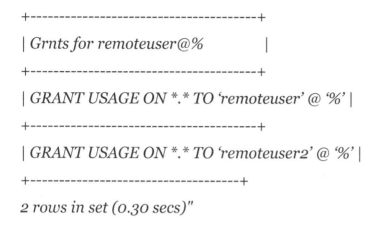

```
+---------------------------------------+
| Grnts for remoteuser@%                |
+---------------------------------------+
| GRANT USAGE ON *.* TO 'remoteuser' @ '%' |
+---------------------------------------+
| GRANT USAGE ON *.* TO 'remoteuser2' @ '%' |
+---------------------------------------+
```

2 rows in set (0.30 secs)"

It is necessary to remember that the single quotation (' ') in the syntax above is particularly significant, if the user accounts have special characters like underscore or percentage.

If you inadvertently cite the user account as usrname@hstname, the server will create new user with the name as usrname@hstname and enables it to start a connection from random hosts, that cannot be anticipated.

The syntax below, for instance, can be used to generate a new accountapi@lclhst that could be connected to the server from random hosts.

CREATE USER 'api@lclhst';

SHOW GRANTS FOR 'api@lclhst';

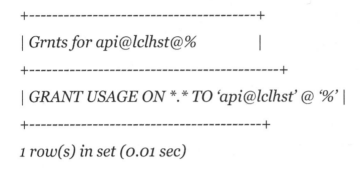

```
+----------------------------------------+
| Grnts for api@lclhst@%                 |
+----------------------------------------+
| GRANT USAGE ON *.* TO 'api@lclhst' @ '%' |
+----------------------------------------+
```

1 row(s) in set (0.01 sec)

If you accidentally generate a user that has already been created in the database, then an error will be issued by MySQL. For instance, the syntax below can be used to generate a new user account called remoteuser:

CREATE USER remoteuser;

The error message below will be displayed on your screen:

ERROR 1398 (HY0000): Action CREATE USER fails for 'remoteuser'@ '%'

It can be noted that the "CREATE USER" statement will only create the new user but not grant any privileges. The GRANT statement can be utilized to give access privileges to the users.

Updating USER PASSWORD

Prior to altering a MySQL user account password, the concerns listed below should be taken into consideration:

- The user account whose password you would like to be modified.
- The applications that are being used with the user account for which you would like to modify the password. If the password is changed without altering the application connection string being used with that user account, then it would be not feasible for those applications to get connected with the database server.

MySQL offers a variety of statements that can be used to alter a user's password, such as UPDATE, SET PASSWORD, and GRANT USAGE statements.

Let's explore some of these syntaxes!

Using UPDATE Statement

The UPDATE can be utilized to make updates to the user tables in the database. You must also execute the "FLUSH PRIVILEGES" statements to refresh privileges from the "grant table," by executing the UPDATE statement.

Assume that you would like to modify the password for the dbadmn user, which links from the local host to the fish. It can be accomplished by executing the query below:

USE msql;

UPDATE usr
SET paswrd = PASWRD ('fish')
WHERE usr = 'dbadmn' AND
  host = 'lclhst';

FLUSH PRIVILEGES;

Using SET PASSWORD Statement

For updating the user password, the user@host format is utilized. Now, imagine that you would like to modify the password for some other user's account, then you will be required to have the UPDATE privilege on your user account.

With the use of the SET PASSOWORD statement, the FLUSH PRIVILEGES statement is not required to be executed, in order to reload privileges to the mysql database from the grant tables.

The syntax below could be utilized to alter the dbadmn user account password:

SET PASSWORD FOR 'dbadmn'@ 'lclhst' = PASSWORD('bigfish');

Using ALTER USER Statement

Another method to update the user password is with the use of the ALTER USER statements with the "IDENTIFIED BY" clause. For instance, the query below can be executed to change the password of the dbadmn user to littlefish.

ALTER USER dbadmn@lclhst IDENTIFY BY 'littlefish';

USEFUL TIP
If you need to change the password of the "root account," then the server must be force quit and started back up without triggering the grant table validation.

Granting User Privileges

As a new user account is created, there are no access privileges afforded to the user by default. The "GRANT" statement must be used in order for granting privileges to all user accounts. The syntax of these statements are shown below:

GRANT priv,[priv], ... ON priv_level
TO usr [IDENTIFIED BY pswrd]
[REQUIRE tssl_optn]
[WITH [GRANT_OPTION | resrce_optn]];

- In the syntax above, we start by specifying one or more privileges following the GRANT clause. Every privilege being granted to the user account must be isolated using a comma, in case you would like to give the user account more than one privilege at the same time. (The list of potential privileges that may be granted to a user account is given in the table below).

- After that you must indicate the "privilege_level" that will determine the levels at which the privilege is applied. The privilege level supported by MySQL are "global (*. *)," "database (database. *)," "table (database.table)" and "column" levels.

- Next you need to indicate the user that needs to be granted the privileges. If the indicated user can be found on the server, then the GRANT statement will modify its privilege. Or else, a new user account will be created by the GRANT statement. The IDENTIFIED BY clause is not mandatory and enables creation of a new password for the user.

- Thereafter, it's indicated if the user needs to start a connection to the database via secured connections.
- At last, the "WITH GRANT OPTION" clause is added which is not mandatory but enables granting and revoking the privileges of other user, that were given to your own account. Moreover, the WITH clause can also be used to assign the resources from the MySQL database server, for example, putting a limit on the number of links or statements that can be used by the user per hour. In shared environments like MySQL shared hosting, the WITH clause is extremely useful.

Note that the GRANT OPTION privilege as well as the privileges you are looking to grant to other users must already be configured to your own user account, so that you are able to use the GRANT statement. If the read only system variable has been allowed, then execution of the GRANT statement requires the SUPER privilege.

PRIVILE-GE	DESCRI-PTION	LEVEL Global	LEVEL Database	LEVEL Table	LEVEL Column	LEVEL Proce-dure	LEVEL Proxy
"ALL"	Granting all privileges at specific access levels except the GRANT OPTION.						
'ALTER'	Allowing users the usage of ALTER TABLE statement.	Y	Y	Y			

"ALTER ROUTINE"	Allowing users to alter and drop saved routines.	Y	Y			Y	
CREATE	Allowing users to generate databases and tables.	Y	Y	Y			
CREATE ROUTINE	Allowing users to create saved routines.	Y	Y				
CREATE TABLESPACE	Allowing users to generate, modify or remove tables and log file groups.	Y					
CREATE TEMPORARY	Allowing users to generate	Y	Y				

TABLES	temp tables with the use of the CREATE TEMPO- RARY TABLE.						
CREATE USER	Allowing users to utilize the CREATE USER, DROP USER, RENAME USER, and REVOKE ALL PRIVI- LEGES state- ments.	Y					
CREATE VIEW	Allowing users to generate	Y	Y	Y			

	or update views.						
DELETE	Allowing users to utilize the DELETE keyword.	Y	Y	Y			
"DROP"	Allowing users to remove databa-ses, tables and views.	Y	Y	Y			
'EVENT'	Enabling the usage of events for the Event Scheduler.	Y	Y				
EXECU-TE	Allowing users for execution of saved routines.	Y	Y	Y			

"FILE"	Allowing users to read the files in the db directories.	Y					
GRANT OPTION	Allowing users privilege for granting or revoking privileges from other users.	Y	Y	Y		Y	Y
'INDEX'	Allowing users to generate or drop indexes.	Y	Y	Y			
INSERT	Allowing users the usage of INSERT state-	Y	Y	Y	Y		

	ments.						
LOCK TABLES	Allowing users the usage of LOCK TABLES on tables that have the SELECT privileges.	**Y**	**Y**				
PRO-CESS	Allowing users to view all processes with SHOW PROCESS -LIST state-ments.	**Y**					
PROXY	Enabling creation of proxy of the users.						

'REFE-RENCES'	Allowing users to generate foreign key.	Y	Y	Y	Y		
RELOAD	Allowing users the usage of the FLUSH operation.	Y					
'REPLI-CATION CLIENT'	Allowing users to query to see where master or slave servers are.	Y					
REPLI-CATION SAVE"	Allowing the users to use replica-ted slaves to read binary	Y					

	log events from the master.						
SELECT	Allowing users the usage of SELECT state-ments.	Y	Y	Y	Y		
"SHOW DATA-BASES"	Allowing users to view all databa-ses.	Y					
"SHOW VIEW"	Allowing users to utilize SHOW CREATE VIEW state-ment.	Y	Y	Y			
"SHUT-DOWN"	Allowing users to use	Y					

	mysqladmin shutdown commands.					
'SUPER'	Allowing users to use other administrative operations such as CHANGE MASTER TO, KILL, PURGE BINARY LOGS, SET GLOBAL and mysqladmin commands.	Y				
'TRIG-GER'	Allowing users the	Y	Y	Y		

	usage of TRIGGER operations						
"UPDATE"	Allowing users the usage of UPDATE statements.	Y	Y	Y	Y		
'USAGE'	Equivalent to no privilege.						

EXAMPLE

More often than not, the CREATE USER statement will be used to first create a new user account and then the GRANT statement is used to assign the user privileges.

For instance, a new super user account can be created by the executing the CREATE USER statement given below:

CREATE USER super@localhost IDENTIFIED BY 'dolphin';

In order to check the privileges granted to the super@localhost user, the query below with SHOW GRANTS statement can be used.

SHOW GRANTS FOR super@localhost;

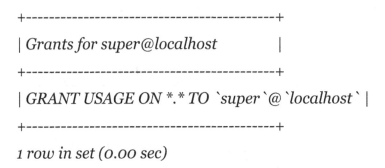

1 row in set (0.00 sec)

Now, if you wanted to assign all privileges to the super@localhost user, the query below with GRANT ALL statement can be used.

GRANT ALL ON *.* TO 'super'@'localhost' WITH GRANT OPTION;

The ON*. * clause refers to all databases and items within those databases. The WITH GRANT OPTION enables super@localhost to assign privileges to other user accounts.

If the SHOW GRANTS statement is used again at this point then it can be seen that privileges of the super@localhost's user have been modified, as shown in the syntax and the result set below:

SHOW GRANTS FOR super@localhost;

```
+----------------------------------------------------------------------+
| Grants for super@localhost                                           |
+----------------------------------------------------------------------+
| GRANT ALL PRIVILEGES ON *.* TO `super`@`localhost`
WITH GRANT OPTION |
+----------------------------------------------------------------------+
```

1 row in set (0.00 sec)

Now, assume that you want to create a new user account with all the server privileges in the *classicmodels* sample database. You can accomplish this by using the query below:

CREATE USER auditor@localhost IDENTIFIED BY 'whale';
GRANT ALL ON classicmodels.* TO auditor@localhost;

Using only one GRANT statement, various privileges can be granted to a user account. For instance, to generate a user account with the privilege of executing SELECT, INSERT and UPDATE statements against the database *classicmodels*, the query below can be used.

CREATE USER rfc IDENTIFIED BY 'shark';

GRANT SELECT, UPDATE, DELETE ON classicmodels.* TO rfc;

Revoking User Privileges

You will be using the MySQL REVOKE statement to revoke the privileges of any user account(s). MySQL enables withdrawal of one or more privileges or even all of the previously granted privileges of a user account.

The query below can be used to revoke particular privileges from a user account:

REVOKE   privilege_type [(column_list)]
*   [, priv_type [(column_list)]]...*
ON [object_type] privilege_level
FROM user [, user]...

In the syntax above, we start by specifying a list of privileges that need to be revoked from a user account next to the REVOKE keyword. YAs you might recall when listing multiple privileges in a statement they must be separated by commas. Then we indicate the privilege level at which the ON clause will be revoking these privileges. Lastly we indicate the user account whose privileges will be revoked in the FROM clause.

Bear in mind that your own user account must have the GRANT OPTION privilege as well as the privileges that you want to revoke from other user accounts.

You will be using the REVOKE statement as shown in the syntax below, if you are looking to withdraw all privileges of a user account:

REVOKE ALL PRIVILEGES, GRANT OPTION FROM user [, user]...

It is important to remember that you are required to have the CREATE USER or the UPDATE privilege at global level for the mysql database, to be able to execute the REVOKE ALL statement.

You will be using the REVOKE PROXY clause as shown in the query below, in order to revoke proxy users:

REVOKE PROXY ON user FROM user [, user]...

A proxy user can be defined as a valid user in MySQL who can impersonate another user. As a result, the proxy user is able to attain all the privileges granted to the user that it is impersonating.

The best practice dictates that you should first check what privileges have been assigned to the user by executing the syntax below with SHOW GRANTS statement, prior to withdrawing the user's privileges:

SHOW GRANTS FOR user;

EXAMPLE

Assume that there is a user named rfd with SELECT, UPDATE and DELETE privileges on the *classicmodels* sample database and you would like to revoke the UPDATE and DELETE privileges from the rfd user. To accomplish this, you can execute the queries below.

To start with we will check the user privileges using the SHOW GRANTS statement below:

SHOW GRANTS FOR rfd;

GRANT SELECT, UPDATE, DELETE ON 'classicmodels'. TO 'rfc'@'%'*

At this point, the UPDATE and REVOKE privileges can be revoked from the rfd user, using the query below:

REVOKE UPDATE, DELETE ON classicmodels.* FROM rfd;

Next, the privileges of the rfd user can be checked with the use of SHOW GRANTS statement.

SHOW GRANTS FOR 'rfd'@'localhost';

GRANT SELECT ON 'classicmodels'.* TO 'rfd'@'%'

Now, if you wanted to revoke all the privileges from the rfd user, you can use the query below:

REVOKE ALL PRIVILEGES, GRANT OPTION FROM rfd;

To verify that all the privileges from the rfd user have been revoked, you will need to use the query below:

SHOW GRANTS FOR rfd;

*GRANT USAGE ON *.* TO 'rfd'@'%'*

Remember, as mentioned in the privileges description table earlier in this book, the USAGE privilege simply means that the user has no privileges in the server.

Resulting Impact of the REVOKE Query

The impact of MySQL REVOKE statement relies primarily on the level of privilege granted to the user account, as explained below:

- The modifications made to the global privileges will only take effect once the user has connected to the MySQL server in a successive session, post the successful execution of the REVOKE query. The modifications will not be applicable to all other users connected to the server, while the REVOKE statement is being executed.
- The modifications made to the database privileges are only applicable once a USE statement has been executed after the execution of the REVOKE query.
- The table and column privilege modifications will be applicable to all the queries executed, after the modifications have been rendered with the REVOKE statement.

Conclusion

Thank you for making it through to the end of **SQL Programming:** *The ultimate guide with exercises, tips and tricks to learn SQL,* Let's hope it was informative and able to provide you with all of the tools you need to achieve your goals whatever they may be.

The next step is to make the best use of your newfound wisdom and learning of the SQL programming language, that will help you gain a powerful entry into the world of data analysis. To make the most of your purchase of this book, I highly recommend that you follow the instructions in this book and install the free and open MySQL user interface on your operating system. This will allow you to get hands-on practice so you will be able to create not only correct but efficient SQL queries to succeed at work and ace those job interview questions. The fundamental element of any kind of learning is repeated practice in order to achieve perfection. So let this book be your personal guide and mentor through the journey of learning SQL programming language for relational database management systems. Another tip to make the best use of this book is to try to come up with your own names and labels to be used within the presented examples and verify those result sets obtained with the ones provided in this book, as you read and understand all the concepts and SQL query structures.

Finally, if you found this book useful in anyway, a review on Amazon is always appreciated!

www.ingramcontent.com/pod-product-compliance
Lightning Source LLC
LaVergne TN
LVHW051228050326
832903LV00028B/2282